# PRODUCTIVITY
## PLANNER

*'Start by doing what's necessary; then do what's possible; and suddenly you are doing the impossible.'*

Francis Of Assisi

*'The way to get started is to quit talking and begin doing.'*

Walt Disney

*'It's not that I'm so smart, it's just that I stay with problems longer.'*

Albert Einstein

*'You were born to win, but to be a winner, you must plan to win, prepare to win, and expect to win.'*

Zig Ziglar

*'Sometimes, things may not go your way, but the effort should be there every single night.'*

Michael Jordan

*'He who is not courageous enough to take risks will accomplish nothing in life.'*

Muhammad Ali

Date: ___ / ___ / 20 _____

# MOST IMPORTANT TASK OF THE DAY
If you only complete this then today was still a great day

1. _____  ○ ○ ○ ○ ○
                             HOW WELL I DID

# TASKS OF SECONDARY IMPORTANCE
Getting these done will make my day even greater

2. _____  ○ ○ ○ ○ ○
                             HOW WELL I DID

3. _____  ○ ○ ○ ○ ○
                             HOW WELL I DID

# ADDITIONAL TASKS
Don't tackle these until the ones above are done

4. _____  ○ ○ ○ ○ ○
                             HOW WELL I DID

5. _____  ○ ○ ○ ○ ○
                             HOW WELL I DID

# NOTES ON MY DAY

_____

_____

_____

## PRODUCTIVITY RATING

1    2    3    4    5    6    7    8    9    10

Date: ___ / ___ / 20 _____

# MOST IMPORTANT TASK OF THE DAY
If you only complete this then today was still a great day

1. _____   ○ ○ ○ ○ ○
                                      HOW WELL I DID

# TASKS OF SECONDARY IMPORTANCE
Getting these done will make my day even greater

2. _____   ○ ○ ○ ○ ○
                                      HOW WELL I DID

3. _____   ○ ○ ○ ○ ○
                                      HOW WELL I DID

# ADDITIONAL TASKS
Don't tackle these until the ones above are done

4. _____   ○ ○ ○ ○ ○
                                      HOW WELL I DID

5. _____   ○ ○ ○ ○ ○
                                      HOW WELL I DID

# NOTES ON MY DAY

_____

_____

_____

### PRODUCTIVITY RATING

1    2    3    4    5    6    7    8    9    10

Date: __ / __ / 20____

# MOST IMPORTANT TASK OF THE DAY
If you only complete this then today was still a great day

1. _____  ◯◯◯◯◯
HOW WELL I DID

# TASKS OF SECONDARY IMPORTANCE
Getting these done will make my day even greater

2. _____  ◯◯◯◯◯
HOW WELL I DID

3. _____  ◯◯◯◯◯
HOW WELL I DID

# ADDITIONAL TASKS
Don't tackle these until the ones above are done

4. _____  ◯◯◯◯◯
HOW WELL I DID

5. _____  ◯◯◯◯◯
HOW WELL I DID

# NOTES ON MY DAY

_____

_____

_____

## PRODUCTIVITY RATING

1    2    3    4    5    6    7    8    9    10

Date: / / 20 _____

# MOST IMPORTANT TASK OF THE DAY
If you only complete this then today was still a great day

1. _____  ◯ ◯ ◯ ◯ ◯
HOW WELL I DID

# TASKS OF SECONDARY IMPORTANCE
Getting these done will make my day even greater

2. _____  ◯ ◯ ◯ ◯ ◯
HOW WELL I DID

3. _____  ◯ ◯ ◯ ◯ ◯
HOW WELL I DID

# ADDITIONAL TASKS
Don't tackle these until the ones above are done

4. _____  ◯ ◯ ◯ ◯ ◯
HOW WELL I DID

5. _____  ◯ ◯ ◯ ◯ ◯
HOW WELL I DID

# NOTES ON MY DAY

_____

_____

_____

**PRODUCTIVITY RATING**

1    2    3    4    5    6    7    8    9    10

Date: ___ / ___ / 20 _____

# MOST IMPORTANT TASK OF THE DAY
If you only complete this then today was still a great day

1. _____    ○ ○ ○ ○ ○
HOW WELL I DID

# TASKS OF SECONDARY IMPORTANCE
Getting these done will make my day even greater

2. _____    ○ ○ ○ ○ ○
HOW WELL I DID

3. _____    ○ ○ ○ ○ ○
HOW WELL I DID

# ADDITIONAL TASKS
Don't tackle these until the ones above are done

4. _____    ○ ○ ○ ○ ○
HOW WELL I DID

5. _____    ○ ○ ○ ○ ○
HOW WELL I DID

# NOTES ON MY DAY

_____

_____

_____

## PRODUCTIVITY RATING

1    2    3    4    5    6    7    8    9    10

# WEEKLY REVIEW

Week of _____

## WEEKLY TRIUMPHS
Want went well this week

_____

_____

_____

## COULD DO BETTER
What fell short of expectations?

_____

_____

_____

## WHAT I'VE LEARNED
Lessons I can grow from

_____

_____

_____

## FOCUS FOR NEXT WEEK
Where I need to spend my energy

_____

_____

## Date: \_\_ / \_\_ / 20 \_\_

# MOST IMPORTANT TASK OF THE DAY
If you only complete this then today was still a great day

1. _____  ◯◯◯◯◯
HOW WELL I DID

# TASKS OF SECONDARY IMPORTANCE
Getting these done will make my day even greater

2. _____  ◯◯◯◯◯
HOW WELL I DID

3. _____  ◯◯◯◯◯
HOW WELL I DID

# ADDITIONAL TASKS
Don't tackle these until the ones above are done

4. _____  ◯◯◯◯◯
HOW WELL I DID

5. _____  ◯◯◯◯◯
HOW WELL I DID

# NOTES ON MY DAY

_____

_____

_____

### PRODUCTIVITY RATING

| 1 | 2 | 3 | 4 | 5 | 6 | 7 | 8 | 9 | 10 |

Date:  /  / 20 ____

# MOST IMPORTANT TASK OF THE DAY
If you only complete this then today was still a great day

1. _____  ○ ○ ○ ○ ○
HOW WELL I DID

# TASKS OF SECONDARY IMPORTANCE
Getting these done will make my day even greater

2. _____  ○ ○ ○ ○ ○
HOW WELL I DID

3. _____  ○ ○ ○ ○ ○
HOW WELL I DID

# ADDITIONAL TASKS
Don't tackle these until the ones above are done

4. _____  ○ ○ ○ ○ ○
HOW WELL I DID

5. _____  ○ ○ ○ ○ ○
HOW WELL I DID

# NOTES ON MY DAY

_____

_____

_____

## PRODUCTIVITY RATING

1    2    3    4    5    6    7    8    9    10

Date: ___ / ___ / 20 _____

# MOST IMPORTANT TASK OF THE DAY
If you only complete this then today was still a great day

1. _____  ◯◯◯◯◯
HOW WELL I DID

# TASKS OF SECONDARY IMPORTANCE
Getting these done will make my day even greater

2. _____  ◯◯◯◯◯
HOW WELL I DID

3. _____  ◯◯◯◯◯
HOW WELL I DID

# ADDITIONAL TASKS
Don't tackle these until the ones above are done

4. _____  ◯◯◯◯◯
HOW WELL I DID

5. _____  ◯◯◯◯◯
HOW WELL I DID

# NOTES ON MY DAY

_____

_____

_____

## PRODUCTIVITY RATING

1     2     3     4     5     6     7     8     9     10

Date: ___ / ___ / 20 ___

# MOST IMPORTANT TASK OF THE DAY

If you only complete this then today was still a great day

1. _____    ○ ○ ○ ○ ○
HOW WELL I DID

# TASKS OF SECONDARY IMPORTANCE

Getting these done will make my day even greater

2. _____    ○ ○ ○ ○ ○
HOW WELL I DID

3. _____    ○ ○ ○ ○ ○
HOW WELL I DID

# ADDITIONAL TASKS

Don't tackle these until the ones above are done

4. _____    ○ ○ ○ ○ ○
HOW WELL I DID

5. _____    ○ ○ ○ ○ ○
HOW WELL I DID

# NOTES ON MY DAY

_____

_____

_____

## PRODUCTIVITY RATING

| 1 | 2 | 3 | 4 | 5 | 6 | 7 | 8 | 9 | 10 |

Date: ___ / ___ / 20 _____

# MOST IMPORTANT TASK OF THE DAY

If you only complete this then today was still a great day

1. _____   ◯ ◯ ◯ ◯ ◯
HOW WELL I DID

# TASKS OF SECONDARY IMPORTANCE

Getting these done will make my day even greater

2. _____   ◯ ◯ ◯ ◯ ◯
HOW WELL I DID

3. _____   ◯ ◯ ◯ ◯ ◯
HOW WELL I DID

# ADDITIONAL TASKS

Don't tackle these until the ones above are done

4. _____   ◯ ◯ ◯ ◯ ◯
HOW WELL I DID

5. _____   ◯ ◯ ◯ ◯ ◯
HOW WELL I DID

# NOTES ON MY DAY

_____

_____

_____

### PRODUCTIVITY RATING

1    2    3    4    5    6    7    8    9    10

# WEEKLY REVIEW

Week of _____

## WEEKLY TRIUMPHS
Want went well this week

_____

_____

_____

## COULD DO BETTER
What fell short of expectations?

_____

_____

_____

## WHAT I'VE LEARNED
Lessons I can grow from

_____

_____

_____

## FOCUS FOR NEXT WEEK
Where I need to spend my energy

_____

_____

Date: ___/___/ 20_____

# MOST IMPORTANT TASK OF THE DAY
If you only complete this then today was still a great day

1. _____  ○ ○ ○ ○ ○
HOW WELL I DID

# TASKS OF SECONDARY IMPORTANCE
Getting these done will make my day even greater

2. _____  ○ ○ ○ ○ ○
HOW WELL I DID

3. _____  ○ ○ ○ ○ ○
HOW WELL I DID

# ADDITIONAL TASKS
Don't tackle these until the ones above are done

4. _____  ○ ○ ○ ○ ○
HOW WELL I DID

5. _____  ○ ○ ○ ○ ○
HOW WELL I DID

# NOTES ON MY DAY

_____

_____

_____

**PRODUCTIVITY RATING**

1    2    3    4    5    6    7    8    9    10

Date: ___ / ___ / 20 ___

# MOST IMPORTANT TASK OF THE DAY
If you only complete this then today was still a great day

1. _____     ◯ ◯ ◯ ◯ ◯
                               HOW WELL I DID

# TASKS OF SECONDARY IMPORTANCE
Getting these done will make my day even greater

2. _____     ◯ ◯ ◯ ◯ ◯
                               HOW WELL I DID

3. _____     ◯ ◯ ◯ ◯ ◯
                               HOW WELL I DID

# ADDITIONAL TASKS
Don't tackle these until the ones above are done

4. _____     ◯ ◯ ◯ ◯ ◯
                               HOW WELL I DID

5. _____     ◯ ◯ ◯ ◯ ◯
                               HOW WELL I DID

# NOTES ON MY DAY

_____

_____

_____

## PRODUCTIVITY RATING
1    2    3    4    5    6    7    8    9    10

Date: / / 20 _____

# MOST IMPORTANT TASK OF THE DAY
If you only complete this then today was still a great day

1. _____  ○ ○ ○ ○ ○
HOW WELL I DID

# TASKS OF SECONDARY IMPORTANCE
Getting these done will make my day even greater

2. _____  ○ ○ ○ ○ ○
HOW WELL I DID

3. _____  ○ ○ ○ ○ ○
HOW WELL I DID

# ADDITIONAL TASKS
Don't tackle these until the ones above are done

4. _____  ○ ○ ○ ○ ○
HOW WELL I DID

5. _____  ○ ○ ○ ○ ○
HOW WELL I DID

# NOTES ON MY DAY

_____

_____

_____

## PRODUCTIVITY RATING

1    2    3    4    5    6    7    8    9    10

Date: ___ / ___ / 20 ___

# MOST IMPORTANT TASK OF THE DAY
If you only complete this then today was still a great day

1. _____  ○○○○○
HOW WELL I DID

# TASKS OF SECONDARY IMPORTANCE
Getting these done will make my day even greater

2. _____  ○○○○○
HOW WELL I DID

3. _____  ○○○○○
HOW WELL I DID

# ADDITIONAL TASKS
Don't tackle these until the ones above are done

4. _____  ○○○○○
HOW WELL I DID

5. _____  ○○○○○
HOW WELL I DID

# NOTES ON MY DAY

_____

_____

_____

## PRODUCTIVITY RATING

1    2    3    4    5    6    7    8    9    10

Date:  /  / 20 _____

# MOST IMPORTANT TASK OF THE DAY
If you only complete this then today was still a great day

○ ○ ○ ○ ○

1. _____
HOW WELL I DID

# TASKS OF SECONDARY IMPORTANCE
Getting these done will make my day even greater

○ ○ ○ ○ ○

2. _____
HOW WELL I DID

○ ○ ○ ○ ○

3. _____
HOW WELL I DID

# ADDITIONAL TASKS
Don't tackle these until the ones above are done

○ ○ ○ ○ ○

4. _____
HOW WELL I DID

○ ○ ○ ○ ○

5. _____
HOW WELL I DID

# NOTES ON MY DAY

_____

_____

_____

## PRODUCTIVITY RATING

| 1 | 2 | 3 | 4 | 5 | 6 | 7 | 8 | 9 | 10 |

# WEEKLY REVIEW

Week of _____

## WEEKLY TRIUMPHS
Want went well this week

_____

_____

_____

## COULD DO BETTER
What fell short of expectations?

_____

_____

_____

## WHAT I'VE LEARNED
Lessons I can grow from

_____

_____

_____

## FOCUS FOR NEXT WEEK
Where I need to spend my energy

_____

_____

Date: ___ / ___ / 20___

# MOST IMPORTANT TASK OF THE DAY
If you only complete this then today was still a great day

○○○○○
1. _____
HOW WELL I DID

# TASKS OF SECONDARY IMPORTANCE
Getting these done will make my day even greater

○○○○○
2. _____
HOW WELL I DID

○○○○○
3. _____
HOW WELL I DID

# ADDITIONAL TASKS
Don't tackle these until the ones above are done

○○○○○
4. _____
HOW WELL I DID

○○○○○
5. _____
HOW WELL I DID

# NOTES ON MY DAY

_____

_____

_____

### PRODUCTIVITY RATING
1    2    3    4    5    6    7    8    9    10

Date: ___ / ___ / 20 _____

# MOST IMPORTANT TASK OF THE DAY

If you only complete this then today was still a great day

1. _____ ○○○○○

HOW WELL I DID

# TASKS OF SECONDARY IMPORTANCE

Getting these done will make my day even greater

2. _____ ○○○○○

HOW WELL I DID

3. _____ ○○○○○

HOW WELL I DID

# ADDITIONAL TASKS

Don't tackle these until the ones above are done

4. _____ ○○○○○

HOW WELL I DID

5. _____ ○○○○○

HOW WELL I DID

# NOTES ON MY DAY

_____

_____

_____

## PRODUCTIVITY RATING

1      2      3      4      5      6      7      8      9      10

Date: __ / __ / 20 _____

# MOST IMPORTANT TASK OF THE DAY
If you only complete this then today was still a great day

1. _____   ◯ ◯ ◯ ◯ ◯
HOW WELL I DID

# TASKS OF SECONDARY IMPORTANCE
Getting these done will make my day even greater

2. _____   ◯ ◯ ◯ ◯ ◯
HOW WELL I DID

3. _____   ◯ ◯ ◯ ◯ ◯
HOW WELL I DID

# ADDITIONAL TASKS
Don't tackle these until the ones above are done

4. _____   ◯ ◯ ◯ ◯ ◯
HOW WELL I DID

5. _____   ◯ ◯ ◯ ◯ ◯
HOW WELL I DID

# NOTES ON MY DAY

_____

_____

_____

## PRODUCTIVITY RATING

| 1 | 2 | 3 | 4 | 5 | 6 | 7 | 8 | 9 | 10 |

Date: / / 20

# MOST IMPORTANT TASK OF THE DAY
If you only complete this then today was still a great day

1. _____  ○ ○ ○ ○ ○
HOW WELL I DID

# TASKS OF SECONDARY IMPORTANCE
Getting these done will make my day even greater

2. _____  ○ ○ ○ ○ ○
HOW WELL I DID

3. _____  ○ ○ ○ ○ ○
HOW WELL I DID

# ADDITIONAL TASKS
Don't tackle these until the ones above are done

4. _____  ○ ○ ○ ○ ○
HOW WELL I DID

5. _____  ○ ○ ○ ○ ○
HOW WELL I DID

# NOTES ON MY DAY

_____

_____

_____

## PRODUCTIVITY RATING

1    2    3    4    5    6    7    8    9    10

Date: / / 20

# MOST IMPORTANT TASK OF THE DAY
If you only complete this then today was still a great day

1. _____   ◯◯◯◯◯
HOW WELL I DID

# TASKS OF SECONDARY IMPORTANCE
Getting these done will make my day even greater

2. _____   ◯◯◯◯◯
HOW WELL I DID

3. _____   ◯◯◯◯◯
HOW WELL I DID

# ADDITIONAL TASKS
Don't tackle these until the ones above are done

4. _____   ◯◯◯◯◯
HOW WELL I DID

5. _____   ◯◯◯◯◯
HOW WELL I DID

# NOTES ON MY DAY

_____

_____

_____

## PRODUCTIVITY RATING

1     2     3     4     5     6     7     8     9     10

# WEEKLY REVIEW

Week of _____

## WEEKLY TRIUMPHS
Want went well this week

_____

_____

_____

## COULD DO BETTER
What fell short of expectations?

_____

_____

_____

## WHAT I'VE LEARNED
Lessons I can grow from

_____

_____

_____

## FOCUS FOR NEXT WEEK
Where I need to spend my energy

_____

_____

Date: / / 20

# MOST IMPORTANT TASK OF THE DAY
If you only complete this then today was still a great day

1. _____  ○○○○○
HOW WELL I DID

# TASKS OF SECONDARY IMPORTANCE
Getting these done will make my day even greater

2. _____  ○○○○○
HOW WELL I DID

3. _____  ○○○○○
HOW WELL I DID

# ADDITIONAL TASKS
Don't tackle these until the ones above are done

4. _____  ○○○○○
HOW WELL I DID

5. _____  ○○○○○
HOW WELL I DID

# NOTES ON MY DAY

_____

_____

_____

**PRODUCTIVITY RATING**

1    2    3    4    5    6    7    8    9    10

Date: __ / __ / 20 __

# MOST IMPORTANT TASK OF THE DAY
If you only complete this then today was still a great day

1. _____   ○○○○○
HOW WELL I DID

# TASKS OF SECONDARY IMPORTANCE
Getting these done will make my day even greater

2. _____   ○○○○○
HOW WELL I DID

3. _____   ○○○○○
HOW WELL I DID

# ADDITIONAL TASKS
Don't tackle these until the ones above are done

4. _____   ○○○○○
HOW WELL I DID

5. _____   ○○○○○
HOW WELL I DID

# NOTES ON MY DAY

_____

_____

_____

**PRODUCTIVITY RATING**

1    2    3    4    5    6    7    8    9    10

Date: / / 20 _____

# MOST IMPORTANT TASK OF THE DAY
If you only complete this then today was still a great day

1. _____  ◯◯◯◯◯
HOW WELL I DID

# TASKS OF SECONDARY IMPORTANCE
Getting these done will make my day even greater

2. _____  ◯◯◯◯◯
HOW WELL I DID

3. _____  ◯◯◯◯◯
HOW WELL I DID

# ADDITIONAL TASKS
Don't tackle these until the ones above are done

4. _____  ◯◯◯◯◯
HOW WELL I DID

5. _____  ◯◯◯◯◯
HOW WELL I DID

# NOTES ON MY DAY

_____

_____

_____

## PRODUCTIVITY RATING

1    2    3    4    5    6    7    8    9    10

Date: _____ / _____ / 20 _____

# MOST IMPORTANT TASK OF THE DAY
If you only complete this then today was still a great day

1. _____    ◯ ◯ ◯ ◯ ◯
HOW WELL I DID

# TASKS OF SECONDARY IMPORTANCE
Getting these done will make my day even greater

2. _____    ◯ ◯ ◯ ◯ ◯
HOW WELL I DID

3. _____    ◯ ◯ ◯ ◯ ◯
HOW WELL I DID

# ADDITIONAL TASKS
Don't tackle these until the ones above are done

4. _____    ◯ ◯ ◯ ◯ ◯
HOW WELL I DID

5. _____    ◯ ◯ ◯ ◯ ◯
HOW WELL I DID

# NOTES ON MY DAY

_____

_____

_____

## PRODUCTIVITY RATING

1    2    3    4    5    6    7    8    9    10

Date:  /  / 20 _____

# MOST IMPORTANT TASK OF THE DAY
If you only complete this then today was still a great day

1. _____  ◯ ◯ ◯ ◯ ◯
HOW WELL I DID

# TASKS OF SECONDARY IMPORTANCE
Getting these done will make my day even greater

2. _____  ◯ ◯ ◯ ◯ ◯
HOW WELL I DID

3. _____  ◯ ◯ ◯ ◯ ◯
HOW WELL I DID

# ADDITIONAL TASKS
Don't tackle these until the ones above are done

4. _____  ◯ ◯ ◯ ◯ ◯
HOW WELL I DID

5. _____  ◯ ◯ ◯ ◯ ◯
HOW WELL I DID

# NOTES ON MY DAY

_____

_____

_____

## PRODUCTIVITY RATING
1    2    3    4    5    6    7    8    9    10

# WEEKLY REVIEW

Week of _____

## WEEKLY TRIUMPHS
Want went well this week

_____

_____

_____

## COULD DO BETTER
What fell short of expectations?

_____

_____

_____

## WHAT I'VE LEARNED
Lessons I can grow from

_____

_____

_____

## FOCUS FOR NEXT WEEK
Where I need to spend my energy

_____

_____

Date:  /  / 20 _____

# MOST IMPORTANT TASK OF THE DAY
If you only complete this then today was still a great day

1. _____  ○○○○○
HOW WELL I DID

# TASKS OF SECONDARY IMPORTANCE
Getting these done will make my day even greater

2. _____  ○○○○○
HOW WELL I DID

3. _____  ○○○○○
HOW WELL I DID

# ADDITIONAL TASKS
Don't tackle these until the ones above are done

4. _____  ○○○○○
HOW WELL I DID

5. _____  ○○○○○
HOW WELL I DID

# NOTES ON MY DAY

_____

_____

_____

**PRODUCTIVITY RATING**

1    2    3    4    5    6    7    8    9    10

Date: / / 20

# MOST IMPORTANT TASK OF THE DAY
If you only complete this then today was still a great day

1. _____    ○○○○○
HOW WELL I DID

# TASKS OF SECONDARY IMPORTANCE
Getting these done will make my day even greater

2. _____    ○○○○○
HOW WELL I DID

3. _____    ○○○○○
HOW WELL I DID

# ADDITIONAL TASKS
Don't tackle these until the ones above are done

4. _____    ○○○○○
HOW WELL I DID

5. _____    ○○○○○
HOW WELL I DID

# NOTES ON MY DAY

_____

_____

_____

**PRODUCTIVITY RATING**

1    2    3    4    5    6    7    8    9    10

Date: __/ / 20__

# MOST IMPORTANT TASK OF THE DAY
If you only complete this then today was still a great day

1. _____

○ ○ ○ ○ ○
HOW WELL I DID

# TASKS OF SECONDARY IMPORTANCE
Getting these done will make my day even greater

2. _____

○ ○ ○ ○ ○
HOW WELL I DID

3. _____

○ ○ ○ ○ ○
HOW WELL I DID

# ADDITIONAL TASKS
Don't tackle these until the ones above are done

4. _____

○ ○ ○ ○ ○
HOW WELL I DID

5. _____

○ ○ ○ ○ ○
HOW WELL I DID

# NOTES ON MY DAY

_____

_____

_____

**PRODUCTIVITY RATING**

1    2    3    4    5    6    7    8    9    10

Date: ___ / ___ / 20 _____

# MOST IMPORTANT TASK OF THE DAY
If you only complete this then today was still a great day

1. _____  ○ ○ ○ ○ ○
HOW WELL I DID

# TASKS OF SECONDARY IMPORTANCE
Getting these done will make my day even greater

2. _____  ○ ○ ○ ○ ○
HOW WELL I DID

3. _____  ○ ○ ○ ○ ○
HOW WELL I DID

# ADDITIONAL TASKS
Don't tackle these until the ones above are done

4. _____  ○ ○ ○ ○ ○
HOW WELL I DID

5. _____  ○ ○ ○ ○ ○
HOW WELL I DID

# NOTES ON MY DAY

_____

_____

_____

## PRODUCTIVITY RATING

1    2    3    4    5    6    7    8    9    10

Date:  /  / 20

# MOST IMPORTANT TASK OF THE DAY
If you only complete this then today was still a great day

1. _____  ○○○○○
HOW WELL I DID

# TASKS OF SECONDARY IMPORTANCE
Getting these done will make my day even greater

2. _____  ○○○○○
HOW WELL I DID

3. _____  ○○○○○
HOW WELL I DID

# ADDITIONAL TASKS
Don't tackle these until the ones above are done

4. _____  ○○○○○
HOW WELL I DID

5. _____  ○○○○○
HOW WELL I DID

# NOTES ON MY DAY

_____

_____

_____

**PRODUCTIVITY RATING**

1    2    3    4    5    6    7    8    9    10

# WEEKLY REVIEW

Week of _____

## WEEKLY TRIUMPHS
Want went well this week

_____

_____

_____

## COULD DO BETTER
What fell short of expectations?

_____

_____

_____

## WHAT I'VE LEARNED
Lessons I can grow from

_____

_____

_____

## FOCUS FOR NEXT WEEK
Where I need to spend my energy

_____

_____

Date: _____ / _____ / 20 _____

# MOST IMPORTANT TASK OF THE DAY
If you only complete this then today was still a great day

1. _____ ○○○○○
HOW WELL I DID

# TASKS OF SECONDARY IMPORTANCE
Getting these done will make my day even greater

2. _____ ○○○○○
HOW WELL I DID

3. _____ ○○○○○
HOW WELL I DID

# ADDITIONAL TASKS
Don't tackle these until the ones above are done

4. _____ ○○○○○
HOW WELL I DID

5. _____ ○○○○○
HOW WELL I DID

# NOTES ON MY DAY

_____

_____

_____

## PRODUCTIVITY RATING

| 1 | 2 | 3 | 4 | 5 | 6 | 7 | 8 | 9 | 10 |

Date: / / 20

# MOST IMPORTANT TASK OF THE DAY
If you only complete this then today was still a great day

1. _____  ○ ○ ○ ○ ○
HOW WELL I DID

# TASKS OF SECONDARY IMPORTANCE
Getting these done will make my day even greater

2. _____  ○ ○ ○ ○ ○
HOW WELL I DID

3. _____  ○ ○ ○ ○ ○
HOW WELL I DID

# ADDITIONAL TASKS
Don't tackle these until the ones above are done

4. _____  ○ ○ ○ ○ ○
HOW WELL I DID

5. _____  ○ ○ ○ ○ ○
HOW WELL I DID

# NOTES ON MY DAY

_____

_____

_____

## PRODUCTIVITY RATING

1    2    3    4    5    6    7    8    9    10

Date: / / 20 _____

# MOST IMPORTANT TASK OF THE DAY

If you only complete this then today was still a great day

○ ○ ○ ○ ○

1. _____

HOW WELL I DID

# TASKS OF SECONDARY IMPORTANCE

Getting these done will make my day even greater

○ ○ ○ ○ ○

2. _____

HOW WELL I DID

○ ○ ○ ○ ○

3. _____

HOW WELL I DID

# ADDITIONAL TASKS

Don't tackle these until the ones above are done

○ ○ ○ ○ ○

4. _____

HOW WELL I DID

○ ○ ○ ○ ○

5. _____

HOW WELL I DID

# NOTES ON MY DAY

_____

_____

_____

## PRODUCTIVITY RATING

1    2    3    4    5    6    7    8    9    10

Date: / / 20

# MOST IMPORTANT TASK OF THE DAY
If you only complete this then today was still a great day

1. _____ ○○○○○
HOW WELL I DID

# TASKS OF SECONDARY IMPORTANCE
Getting these done will make my day even greater

2. _____ ○○○○○
HOW WELL I DID

3. _____ ○○○○○
HOW WELL I DID

# ADDITIONAL TASKS
Don't tackle these until the ones above are done

4. _____ ○○○○○
HOW WELL I DID

5. _____ ○○○○○
HOW WELL I DID

# NOTES ON MY DAY

_____

_____

_____

## PRODUCTIVITY RATING

1    2    3    4    5    6    7    8    9    10

Date: ___ / ___ / 20 _____

# MOST IMPORTANT TASK OF THE DAY
If you only complete this then today was still a great day

1. _____   ○ ○ ○ ○ ○
HOW WELL I DID

# TASKS OF SECONDARY IMPORTANCE
Getting these done will make my day even greater

2. _____   ○ ○ ○ ○ ○
HOW WELL I DID

3. _____   ○ ○ ○ ○ ○
HOW WELL I DID

# ADDITIONAL TASKS
Don't tackle these until the ones above are done

4. _____   ○ ○ ○ ○ ○
HOW WELL I DID

5. _____   ○ ○ ○ ○ ○
HOW WELL I DID

# NOTES ON MY DAY

_____

_____

_____

## PRODUCTIVITY RATING

1    2    3    4    5    6    7    8    9    10

# WEEKLY REVIEW

Week of _____

## WEEKLY TRIUMPHS
Want went well this week

_____

_____

_____

## COULD DO BETTER
What fell short of expectations?

_____

_____

_____

## WHAT I'VE LEARNED
Lessons I can grow from

_____

_____

_____

## FOCUS FOR NEXT WEEK
Where I need to spend my energy

_____

_____

Date: ___ / ___ / 20 ___

# MOST IMPORTANT TASK OF THE DAY
If you only complete this then today was still a great day

1. _____  ◯◯◯◯◯
HOW WELL I DID

# TASKS OF SECONDARY IMPORTANCE
Getting these done will make my day even greater

2. _____  ◯◯◯◯◯
HOW WELL I DID

3. _____  ◯◯◯◯◯
HOW WELL I DID

# ADDITIONAL TASKS
Don't tackle these until the ones above are done

4. _____  ◯◯◯◯◯
HOW WELL I DID

5. _____  ◯◯◯◯◯
HOW WELL I DID

# NOTES ON MY DAY

_____

_____

_____

### PRODUCTIVITY RATING

1    2    3    4    5    6    7    8    9    10

Date: ___ / ___ / 20 ___

# MOST IMPORTANT TASK OF THE DAY

If you only complete this then today was still a great day

1. _____  ○○○○○
HOW WELL I DID

# TASKS OF SECONDARY IMPORTANCE

Getting these done will make my day even greater

2. _____  ○○○○○
HOW WELL I DID

3. _____  ○○○○○
HOW WELL I DID

# ADDITIONAL TASKS

Don't tackle these until the ones above are done

4. _____  ○○○○○
HOW WELL I DID

5. _____  ○○○○○
HOW WELL I DID

# NOTES ON MY DAY

_____

_____

_____

## PRODUCTIVITY RATING

1    2    3    4    5    6    7    8    9    10

Date: ___ / ___ / 20_____

# MOST IMPORTANT TASK OF THE DAY
If you only complete this then today was still a great day

1. _____  ◯ ◯ ◯ ◯ ◯
HOW WELL I DID

# TASKS OF SECONDARY IMPORTANCE
Getting these done will make my day even greater

2. _____  ◯ ◯ ◯ ◯ ◯
HOW WELL I DID

3. _____  ◯ ◯ ◯ ◯ ◯
HOW WELL I DID

# ADDITIONAL TASKS
Don't tackle these until the ones above are done

4. _____  ◯ ◯ ◯ ◯ ◯
HOW WELL I DID

5. _____  ◯ ◯ ◯ ◯ ◯
HOW WELL I DID

# NOTES ON MY DAY

_____

_____

_____

## PRODUCTIVITY RATING

| 1 | 2 | 3 | 4 | 5 | 6 | 7 | 8 | 9 | 10 |

Date: __ / __ / 20 ____

# MOST IMPORTANT TASK OF THE DAY
If you only complete this then today was still a great day

1. _____  ◯ ◯ ◯ ◯ ◯
HOW WELL I DID

# TASKS OF SECONDARY IMPORTANCE
Getting these done will make my day even greater

2. _____  ◯ ◯ ◯ ◯ ◯
HOW WELL I DID

3. _____  ◯ ◯ ◯ ◯ ◯
HOW WELL I DID

# ADDITIONAL TASKS
Don't tackle these until the ones above are done

4. _____  ◯ ◯ ◯ ◯ ◯
HOW WELL I DID

5. _____  ◯ ◯ ◯ ◯ ◯
HOW WELL I DID

# NOTES ON MY DAY

_____

_____

_____

## PRODUCTIVITY RATING

1    2    3    4    5    6    7    8    9    10

Date: ___ / ___ / 20 _____

# MOST IMPORTANT TASK OF THE DAY
If you only complete this then today was still a great day

1. _____  ◯ ◯ ◯ ◯ ◯
                                    HOW WELL I DID

# TASKS OF SECONDARY IMPORTANCE
Getting these done will make my day even greater

2. _____  ◯ ◯ ◯ ◯ ◯
                                    HOW WELL I DID

3. _____  ◯ ◯ ◯ ◯ ◯
                                    HOW WELL I DID

# ADDITIONAL TASKS
Don't tackle these until the ones above are done

4. _____  ◯ ◯ ◯ ◯ ◯
                                    HOW WELL I DID

5. _____  ◯ ◯ ◯ ◯ ◯
                                    HOW WELL I DID

# NOTES ON MY DAY

_____

_____

_____

## PRODUCTIVITY RATING

1    2    3    4    5    6    7    8    9    10

# WEEKLY REVIEW

Week of _____

## WEEKLY TRIUMPHS
Want went well this week

_____

_____

_____

## COULD DO BETTER
What fell short of expectations?

_____

_____

_____

## WHAT I'VE LEARNED
Lessons I can grow from

_____

_____

_____

## FOCUS FOR NEXT WEEK
Where I need to spend my energy

_____

_____

Date: __ / __ / 20 ____

# MOST IMPORTANT TASK OF THE DAY
If you only complete this then today was still a great day

1. _____   ◯ ◯ ◯ ◯ ◯
HOW WELL I DID

# TASKS OF SECONDARY IMPORTANCE
Getting these done will make my day even greater

2. _____   ◯ ◯ ◯ ◯ ◯
HOW WELL I DID

3. _____   ◯ ◯ ◯ ◯ ◯
HOW WELL I DID

# ADDITIONAL TASKS
Don't tackle these until the ones above are done

4. _____   ◯ ◯ ◯ ◯ ◯
HOW WELL I DID

5. _____   ◯ ◯ ◯ ◯ ◯
HOW WELL I DID

# NOTES ON MY DAY

_____

_____

_____

**PRODUCTIVITY RATING**

| 1 | 2 | 3 | 4 | 5 | 6 | 7 | 8 | 9 | 10 |

Date:  /  / 20

# MOST IMPORTANT TASK OF THE DAY
If you only complete this then today was still a great day

1. _____  ◯◯◯◯◯
HOW WELL I DID

# TASKS OF SECONDARY IMPORTANCE
Getting these done will make my day even greater

2. _____  ◯◯◯◯◯
HOW WELL I DID

3. _____  ◯◯◯◯◯
HOW WELL I DID

# ADDITIONAL TASKS
Don't tackle these until the ones above are done

4. _____  ◯◯◯◯◯
HOW WELL I DID

5. _____  ◯◯◯◯◯
HOW WELL I DID

# NOTES ON MY DAY

_____

_____

_____

## PRODUCTIVITY RATING

1    2    3    4    5    6    7    8    9    10

Date: ___ / ___ / 20 _____

# MOST IMPORTANT TASK OF THE DAY
If you only complete this then today was still a great day

1. _____  ○ ○ ○ ○ ○
HOW WELL I DID

# TASKS OF SECONDARY IMPORTANCE
Getting these done will make my day even greater

2. _____  ○ ○ ○ ○ ○
HOW WELL I DID

3. _____  ○ ○ ○ ○ ○
HOW WELL I DID

# ADDITIONAL TASKS
Don't tackle these until the ones above are done

4. _____  ○ ○ ○ ○ ○
HOW WELL I DID

5. _____  ○ ○ ○ ○ ○
HOW WELL I DID

# NOTES ON MY DAY

_____

_____

_____

## PRODUCTIVITY RATING

1    2    3    4    5    6    7    8    9    10

Date: ___ / ___ / 20 _____

# MOST IMPORTANT TASK OF THE DAY

If you only complete this then today was still a great day

1. _____ ○ ○ ○ ○ ○

HOW WELL I DID

# TASKS OF SECONDARY IMPORTANCE

Getting these done will make my day even greater

2. _____ ○ ○ ○ ○ ○

HOW WELL I DID

3. _____ ○ ○ ○ ○ ○

HOW WELL I DID

# ADDITIONAL TASKS

Don't tackle these until the ones above are done

4. _____ ○ ○ ○ ○ ○

HOW WELL I DID

5. _____ ○ ○ ○ ○ ○

HOW WELL I DID

# NOTES ON MY DAY

_____

_____

_____

## PRODUCTIVITY RATING

| 1 | 2 | 3 | 4 | 5 | 6 | 7 | 8 | 9 | 10 |

Date: / / 20

# MOST IMPORTANT TASK OF THE DAY
If you only complete this then today was still a great day

1. _____  ◯◯◯◯◯
HOW WELL I DID

# TASKS OF SECONDARY IMPORTANCE
Getting these done will make my day even greater

2. _____  ◯◯◯◯◯
HOW WELL I DID

3. _____  ◯◯◯◯◯
HOW WELL I DID

# ADDITIONAL TASKS
Don't tackle these until the ones above are done

4. _____  ◯◯◯◯◯
HOW WELL I DID

5. _____  ◯◯◯◯◯
HOW WELL I DID

# NOTES ON MY DAY

_____

_____

_____

## PRODUCTIVITY RATING

1    2    3    4    5    6    7    8    9    10

# WEEKLY REVIEW

Week of _____

## WEEKLY TRIUMPHS
Want went well this week

_____

_____

_____

## COULD DO BETTER
What fell short of expectations?

_____

_____

_____

## WHAT I'VE LEARNED
Lessons I can grow from

_____

_____

_____

## FOCUS FOR NEXT WEEK
Where I need to spend my energy

_____

_____

Date: / / 20

# MOST IMPORTANT TASK OF THE DAY
If you only complete this then today was still a great day

1. _____  ○ ○ ○ ○ ○
HOW WELL I DID

# TASKS OF SECONDARY IMPORTANCE
Getting these done will make my day even greater

2. _____  ○ ○ ○ ○ ○
HOW WELL I DID

3. _____  ○ ○ ○ ○ ○
HOW WELL I DID

# ADDITIONAL TASKS
Don't tackle these until the ones above are done

4. _____  ○ ○ ○ ○ ○
HOW WELL I DID

5. _____  ○ ○ ○ ○ ○
HOW WELL I DID

# NOTES ON MY DAY

_____

_____

_____

## PRODUCTIVITY RATING

1        2        3        4        5        6        7        8        9        10

Date: / / 20

# MOST IMPORTANT TASK OF THE DAY
If you only complete this then today was still a great day

1. _____ ○○○○○
HOW WELL I DID

# TASKS OF SECONDARY IMPORTANCE
Getting these done will make my day even greater

2. _____ ○○○○○
HOW WELL I DID

3. _____ ○○○○○
HOW WELL I DID

# ADDITIONAL TASKS
Don't tackle these until the ones above are done

4. _____ ○○○○○
HOW WELL I DID

5. _____ ○○○○○
HOW WELL I DID

# NOTES ON MY DAY

_____

_____

_____

## PRODUCTIVITY RATING

1    2    3    4    5    6    7    8    9    10

Date: ___/___/ 20_____

# MOST IMPORTANT TASK OF THE DAY
If you only complete this then today was still a great day

1. _____        ○○○○○
                                             HOW WELL I DID

# TASKS OF SECONDARY IMPORTANCE
Getting these done will make my day even greater

2. _____        ○○○○○
                                             HOW WELL I DID

3. _____        ○○○○○
                                             HOW WELL I DID

# ADDITIONAL TASKS
Don't tackle these until the ones above are done

4. _____        ○○○○○
                                             HOW WELL I DID

5. _____        ○○○○○
                                             HOW WELL I DID

# NOTES ON MY DAY

_____

_____

_____

## PRODUCTIVITY RATING

1    2    3    4    5    6    7    8    9    10

Date:  /  / 20

# MOST IMPORTANT TASK OF THE DAY
If you only complete this then today was still a great day

1. _____  ◯◯◯◯◯
HOW WELL I DID

# TASKS OF SECONDARY IMPORTANCE
Getting these done will make my day even greater

2. _____  ◯◯◯◯◯
HOW WELL I DID

3. _____  ◯◯◯◯◯
HOW WELL I DID

# ADDITIONAL TASKS
Don't tackle these until the ones above are done

4. _____  ◯◯◯◯◯
HOW WELL I DID

5. _____  ◯◯◯◯◯
HOW WELL I DID

# NOTES ON MY DAY

_____

_____

_____

## PRODUCTIVITY RATING

1    2    3    4    5    6    7    8    9    10

Date:  /  / 20 _____

# MOST IMPORTANT TASK OF THE DAY
If you only complete this then today was still a great day

◯ ◯ ◯ ◯ ◯

1. _____

HOW WELL I DID

# TASKS OF SECONDARY IMPORTANCE
Getting these done will make my day even greater

◯ ◯ ◯ ◯ ◯

2. _____

HOW WELL I DID

◯ ◯ ◯ ◯ ◯

3. _____

HOW WELL I DID

# ADDITIONAL TASKS
Don't tackle these until the ones above are done

◯ ◯ ◯ ◯ ◯

4. _____

HOW WELL I DID

◯ ◯ ◯ ◯ ◯

5. _____

HOW WELL I DID

# NOTES ON MY DAY

_____

_____

_____

## PRODUCTIVITY RATING

1    2    3    4    5    6    7    8    9    10

# WEEKLY REVIEW

Week of _____

## WEEKLY TRIUMPHS
Want went well this week

_____

_____

_____

## COULD DO BETTER
What fell short of expectations?

_____

_____

_____

## WHAT I'VE LEARNED
Lessons I can grow from

_____

_____

_____

## FOCUS FOR NEXT WEEK
Where I need to spend my energy

_____

_____

## Date: ___ / ___ / 20 ___

# MOST IMPORTANT TASK OF THE DAY
If you only complete this then today was still a great day

1. _____  ◯ ◯ ◯ ◯ ◯
                                      HOW WELL I DID

# TASKS OF SECONDARY IMPORTANCE
Getting these done will make my day even greater

2. _____  ◯ ◯ ◯ ◯ ◯
                                      HOW WELL I DID

3. _____  ◯ ◯ ◯ ◯ ◯
                                      HOW WELL I DID

# ADDITIONAL TASKS
Don't tackle these until the ones above are done

4. _____  ◯ ◯ ◯ ◯ ◯
                                      HOW WELL I DID

5. _____  ◯ ◯ ◯ ◯ ◯
                                      HOW WELL I DID

# NOTES ON MY DAY

_____

_____

_____

### PRODUCTIVITY RATING

| 1 | 2 | 3 | 4 | 5 | 6 | 7 | 8 | 9 | 10 |

Date: ___ / ___ / 20 _____

# MOST IMPORTANT TASK OF THE DAY
If you only complete this then today was still a great day

1. _____   ○ ○ ○ ○ ○
                                        HOW WELL I DID

# TASKS OF SECONDARY IMPORTANCE
Getting these done will make my day even greater

2. _____   ○ ○ ○ ○ ○
                                        HOW WELL I DID

3. _____   ○ ○ ○ ○ ○
                                        HOW WELL I DID

# ADDITIONAL TASKS
Don't tackle these until the ones above are done

4. _____   ○ ○ ○ ○ ○
                                        HOW WELL I DID

5. _____   ○ ○ ○ ○ ○
                                        HOW WELL I DID

# NOTES ON MY DAY

_____

_____

_____

## PRODUCTIVITY RATING

1    2    3    4    5    6    7    8    9    10

Date:  /  / 20

# MOST IMPORTANT TASK OF THE DAY
If you only complete this then today was still a great day

1. _____  ◯◯◯◯◯
HOW WELL I DID

# TASKS OF SECONDARY IMPORTANCE
Getting these done will make my day even greater

2. _____  ◯◯◯◯◯
HOW WELL I DID

3. _____  ◯◯◯◯◯
HOW WELL I DID

# ADDITIONAL TASKS
Don't tackle these until the ones above are done

4. _____  ◯◯◯◯◯
HOW WELL I DID

5. _____  ◯◯◯◯◯
HOW WELL I DID

# NOTES ON MY DAY

_____

_____

_____

## PRODUCTIVITY RATING

1    2    3    4    5    6    7    8    9    10

Date:  /  / 20

# MOST IMPORTANT TASK OF THE DAY
If you only complete this then today was still a great day

1. _____  ○○○○○
HOW WELL I DID

# TASKS OF SECONDARY IMPORTANCE
Getting these done will make my day even greater

2. _____  ○○○○○
HOW WELL I DID

3. _____  ○○○○○
HOW WELL I DID

# ADDITIONAL TASKS
Don't tackle these until the ones above are done

4. _____  ○○○○○
HOW WELL I DID

5. _____  ○○○○○
HOW WELL I DID

# NOTES ON MY DAY

_____

_____

_____

## PRODUCTIVITY RATING

1    2    3    4    5    6    7    8    9    10

Date:  /  / 20

# MOST IMPORTANT TASK OF THE DAY
If you only complete this then today was still a great day

○○○○○
1. _____
HOW WELL I DID

# TASKS OF SECONDARY IMPORTANCE
Getting these done will make my day even greater

○○○○○
2. _____
HOW WELL I DID

○○○○○
3. _____
HOW WELL I DID

# ADDITIONAL TASKS
Don't tackle these until the ones above are done

○○○○○
4. _____
HOW WELL I DID

○○○○○
5. _____
HOW WELL I DID

# NOTES ON MY DAY

_____

_____

_____

## PRODUCTIVITY RATING
1    2    3    4    5    6    7    8    9    10

# WEEKLY REVIEW

Week of _____

## WEEKLY TRIUMPHS
Want went well this week

_____

_____

_____

## COULD DO BETTER
What fell short of expectations?

_____

_____

_____

## WHAT I'VE LEARNED
Lessons I can grow from

_____

_____

_____

## FOCUS FOR NEXT WEEK
Where I need to spend my energy

_____

_____

Date:  /  / 20 _____

# MOST IMPORTANT TASK OF THE DAY
If you only complete this then today was still a great day

○ ○ ○ ○ ○

1. _____
HOW WELL I DID

# TASKS OF SECONDARY IMPORTANCE
Getting these done will make my day even greater

○ ○ ○ ○ ○

2. _____
HOW WELL I DID

○ ○ ○ ○ ○

3. _____
HOW WELL I DID

# ADDITIONAL TASKS
Don't tackle these until the ones above are done

○ ○ ○ ○ ○

4. _____
HOW WELL I DID

○ ○ ○ ○ ○

5. _____
HOW WELL I DID

# NOTES ON MY DAY

_____

_____

_____

## PRODUCTIVITY RATING

| 1 | 2 | 3 | 4 | 5 | 6 | 7 | 8 | 9 | 10 |

Date: __/ __/ 20____

# MOST IMPORTANT TASK OF THE DAY
If you only complete this then today was still a great day

1. _____    ○ ○ ○ ○ ○
                               HOW WELL I DID

# TASKS OF SECONDARY IMPORTANCE
Getting these done will make my day even greater

2. _____    ○ ○ ○ ○ ○
                               HOW WELL I DID

3. _____    ○ ○ ○ ○ ○
                               HOW WELL I DID

# ADDITIONAL TASKS
Don't tackle these until the ones above are done

4. _____    ○ ○ ○ ○ ○
                               HOW WELL I DID

5. _____    ○ ○ ○ ○ ○
                               HOW WELL I DID

# NOTES ON MY DAY

_____

_____

_____

## PRODUCTIVITY RATING
1    2    3    4    5    6    7    8    9    10

Date: / / 20

# MOST IMPORTANT TASK OF THE DAY
If you only complete this then today was still a great day

1. _____  ◯◯◯◯◯
HOW WELL I DID

# TASKS OF SECONDARY IMPORTANCE
Getting these done will make my day even greater

2. _____  ◯◯◯◯◯
HOW WELL I DID

3. _____  ◯◯◯◯◯
HOW WELL I DID

# ADDITIONAL TASKS
Don't tackle these until the ones above are done

4. _____  ◯◯◯◯◯
HOW WELL I DID

5. _____  ◯◯◯◯◯
HOW WELL I DID

# NOTES ON MY DAY

_____

_____

_____

**PRODUCTIVITY RATING**

1    2    3    4    5    6    7    8    9    10

Date: __ / __ / 20____

# MOST IMPORTANT TASK OF THE DAY
If you only complete this then today was still a great day

1. _____ ○○○○○
HOW WELL I DID

# TASKS OF SECONDARY IMPORTANCE
Getting these done will make my day even greater

2. _____ ○○○○○
HOW WELL I DID

3. _____ ○○○○○
HOW WELL I DID

# ADDITIONAL TASKS
Don't tackle these until the ones above are done

4. _____ ○○○○○
HOW WELL I DID

5. _____ ○○○○○
HOW WELL I DID

# NOTES ON MY DAY

_____

_____

_____

## PRODUCTIVITY RATING

1    2    3    4    5    6    7    8    9    10

Date:  /  / 20 _____

# MOST IMPORTANT TASK OF THE DAY
If you only complete this then today was still a great day

○ ○ ○ ○ ○

1. _____

HOW WELL I DID

# TASKS OF SECONDARY IMPORTANCE
Getting these done will make my day even greater

○ ○ ○ ○ ○

2. _____

HOW WELL I DID

○ ○ ○ ○ ○

3. _____

HOW WELL I DID

# ADDITIONAL TASKS
Don't tackle these until the ones above are done

○ ○ ○ ○ ○

4. _____

HOW WELL I DID

○ ○ ○ ○ ○

5. _____

HOW WELL I DID

# NOTES ON MY DAY

_____

_____

_____

## PRODUCTIVITY RATING

| 1 | 2 | 3 | 4 | 5 | 6 | 7 | 8 | 9 | 10 |

# WEEKLY REVIEW

Week of _____

## WEEKLY TRIUMPHS
Want went well this week

_____

_____

_____

## COULD DO BETTER
What fell short of expectations?

_____

_____

_____

## WHAT I'VE LEARNED
Lessons I can grow from

_____

_____

_____

## FOCUS FOR NEXT WEEK
Where I need to spend my energy

_____

_____

Date: ___ / ___ / 20 ___

# MOST IMPORTANT TASK OF THE DAY
If you only complete this then today was still a great day

1. _____     ○ ○ ○ ○ ○
                               HOW WELL I DID

# TASKS OF SECONDARY IMPORTANCE
Getting these done will make my day even greater

2. _____     ○ ○ ○ ○ ○
                               HOW WELL I DID

3. _____     ○ ○ ○ ○ ○
                               HOW WELL I DID

# ADDITIONAL TASKS
Don't tackle these until the ones above are done

4. _____     ○ ○ ○ ○ ○
                               HOW WELL I DID

5. _____     ○ ○ ○ ○ ○
                               HOW WELL I DID

# NOTES ON MY DAY

_____

_____

_____

## PRODUCTIVITY RATING

1     2     3     4     5     6     7     8     9     10

Date:  /  / 20

# MOST IMPORTANT TASK OF THE DAY
If you only complete this then today was still a great day

1. _____  ○○○○○
HOW WELL I DID

# TASKS OF SECONDARY IMPORTANCE
Getting these done will make my day even greater

2. _____  ○○○○○
HOW WELL I DID

3. _____  ○○○○○
HOW WELL I DID

# ADDITIONAL TASKS
Don't tackle these until the ones above are done

4. _____  ○○○○○
HOW WELL I DID

5. _____  ○○○○○
HOW WELL I DID

# NOTES ON MY DAY

_____

_____

_____

## PRODUCTIVITY RATING
1    2    3    4    5    6    7    8    9    10

Date: ___/___/20 _____

# MOST IMPORTANT TASK OF THE DAY
If you only complete this then today was still a great day

1. _____  ○ ○ ○ ○ ○
HOW WELL I DID

# TASKS OF SECONDARY IMPORTANCE
Getting these done will make my day even greater

2. _____  ○ ○ ○ ○ ○
HOW WELL I DID

3. _____  ○ ○ ○ ○ ○
HOW WELL I DID

# ADDITIONAL TASKS
Don't tackle these until the ones above are done

4. _____  ○ ○ ○ ○ ○
HOW WELL I DID

5. _____  ○ ○ ○ ○ ○
HOW WELL I DID

# NOTES ON MY DAY

_____

_____

_____

## PRODUCTIVITY RATING

1    2    3    4    5    6    7    8    9    10

Date: ___ / ___ / 20 _____

# MOST IMPORTANT TASK OF THE DAY
If you only complete this then today was still a great day

1. _____  ◯◯◯◯◯
HOW WELL I DID

# TASKS OF SECONDARY IMPORTANCE
Getting these done will make my day even greater

2. _____  ◯◯◯◯◯
HOW WELL I DID

3. _____  ◯◯◯◯◯
HOW WELL I DID

# ADDITIONAL TASKS
Don't tackle these until the ones above are done

4. _____  ◯◯◯◯◯
HOW WELL I DID

5. _____  ◯◯◯◯◯
HOW WELL I DID

# NOTES ON MY DAY

_____

_____

_____

## PRODUCTIVITY RATING

1    2    3    4    5    6    7    8    9    10

Date: ___ / ___ / 20 _____

# MOST IMPORTANT TASK OF THE DAY
If you only complete this then today was still a great day

○ ○ ○ ○ ○

1. _____
HOW WELL I DID

# TASKS OF SECONDARY IMPORTANCE
Getting these done will make my day even greater

○ ○ ○ ○ ○

2. _____
HOW WELL I DID

○ ○ ○ ○ ○

3. _____
HOW WELL I DID

# ADDITIONAL TASKS
Don't tackle these until the ones above are done

○ ○ ○ ○ ○

4. _____
HOW WELL I DID

○ ○ ○ ○ ○

5. _____
HOW WELL I DID

# NOTES ON MY DAY

_____

_____

_____

### PRODUCTIVITY RATING

1    2    3    4    5    6    7    8    9    10

# WEEKLY REVIEW

Week of _____

## WEEKLY TRIUMPHS
Want went well this week

_____

_____

_____

## COULD DO BETTER
What fell short of expectations?

_____

_____

_____

## WHAT I'VE LEARNED
Lessons I can grow from

_____

_____

_____

## FOCUS FOR NEXT WEEK
Where I need to spend my energy

_____

_____

Date: __ / __ / 20 ____

# MOST IMPORTANT TASK OF THE DAY
If you only complete this then today was still a great day

1. _____    ◯ ◯ ◯ ◯ ◯
HOW WELL I DID

# TASKS OF SECONDARY IMPORTANCE
Getting these done will make my day even greater

2. _____    ◯ ◯ ◯ ◯ ◯
HOW WELL I DID

3. _____    ◯ ◯ ◯ ◯ ◯
HOW WELL I DID

# ADDITIONAL TASKS
Don't tackle these until the ones above are done

4. _____    ◯ ◯ ◯ ◯ ◯
HOW WELL I DID

5. _____    ◯ ◯ ◯ ◯ ◯
HOW WELL I DID

# NOTES ON MY DAY

_____

_____

_____

**PRODUCTIVITY RATING**

1    2    3    4    5    6    7    8    9    10

Date: ___/___/20_____

# MOST IMPORTANT TASK OF THE DAY

If you only complete this then today was still a great day

1. _____  ◯ ◯ ◯ ◯ ◯
HOW WELL I DID

# TASKS OF SECONDARY IMPORTANCE

Getting these done will make my day even greater

2. _____  ◯ ◯ ◯ ◯ ◯
HOW WELL I DID

3. _____  ◯ ◯ ◯ ◯ ◯
HOW WELL I DID

# ADDITIONAL TASKS

Don't tackle these until the ones above are done

4. _____  ◯ ◯ ◯ ◯ ◯
HOW WELL I DID

5. _____  ◯ ◯ ◯ ◯ ◯
HOW WELL I DID

# NOTES ON MY DAY

_____

_____

_____

## PRODUCTIVITY RATING

1    2    3    4    5    6    7    8    9    10

Date: ___ / ___ / 20 _____

# MOST IMPORTANT TASK OF THE DAY
If you only complete this then today was still a great day

1. _____     ○ ○ ○ ○ ○
                               HOW WELL I DID

# TASKS OF SECONDARY IMPORTANCE
Getting these done will make my day even greater

2. _____     ○ ○ ○ ○ ○
                               HOW WELL I DID

3. _____     ○ ○ ○ ○ ○
                               HOW WELL I DID

# ADDITIONAL TASKS
Don't tackle these until the ones above are done

4. _____     ○ ○ ○ ○ ○
                               HOW WELL I DID

5. _____     ○ ○ ○ ○ ○
                               HOW WELL I DID

# NOTES ON MY DAY

_____

_____

_____

**PRODUCTIVITY RATING**

1    2    3    4    5    6    7    8    9    10

Date: ___ / ___ / 20 _____

# MOST IMPORTANT TASK OF THE DAY
If you only complete this then today was still a great day

1. _____  ○ ○ ○ ○ ○
HOW WELL I DID

# TASKS OF SECONDARY IMPORTANCE
Getting these done will make my day even greater

2. _____  ○ ○ ○ ○ ○
HOW WELL I DID

3. _____  ○ ○ ○ ○ ○
HOW WELL I DID

# ADDITIONAL TASKS
Don't tackle these until the ones above are done

4. _____  ○ ○ ○ ○ ○
HOW WELL I DID

5. _____  ○ ○ ○ ○ ○
HOW WELL I DID

# NOTES ON MY DAY

_____

_____

_____

## PRODUCTIVITY RATING

| 1 | 2 | 3 | 4 | 5 | 6 | 7 | 8 | 9 | 10 |

Date: ___/___/20_____

# MOST IMPORTANT TASK OF THE DAY
If you only complete this then today was still a great day

1. _____     ○○○○○
                                  HOW WELL I DID

# TASKS OF SECONDARY IMPORTANCE
Getting these done will make my day even greater

2. _____     ○○○○○
                                  HOW WELL I DID

3. _____     ○○○○○
                                  HOW WELL I DID

# ADDITIONAL TASKS
Don't tackle these until the ones above are done

4. _____     ○○○○○
                                  HOW WELL I DID

5. _____     ○○○○○
                                  HOW WELL I DID

# NOTES ON MY DAY

_____

_____

_____

### PRODUCTIVITY RATING

1    2    3    4    5    6    7    8    9    10

# WEEKLY REVIEW

Week of _____

## WEEKLY TRIUMPHS
Want went well this week

_____

_____

_____

## COULD DO BETTER
What fell short of expectations?

_____

_____

_____

## WHAT I'VE LEARNED
Lessons I can grow from

_____

_____

_____

## FOCUS FOR NEXT WEEK
Where I need to spend my energy

_____

_____

Date: ___ / ___ / 20 _____

# MOST IMPORTANT TASK OF THE DAY
If you only complete this then today was still a great day

1. _____  ○ ○ ○ ○ ○
HOW WELL I DID

# TASKS OF SECONDARY IMPORTANCE
Getting these done will make my day even greater

2. _____  ○ ○ ○ ○ ○
HOW WELL I DID

3. _____  ○ ○ ○ ○ ○
HOW WELL I DID

# ADDITIONAL TASKS
Don't tackle these until the ones above are done

4. _____  ○ ○ ○ ○ ○
HOW WELL I DID

5. _____  ○ ○ ○ ○ ○
HOW WELL I DID

# NOTES ON MY DAY

_____

_____

_____

## PRODUCTIVITY RATING

| 1 | 2 | 3 | 4 | 5 | 6 | 7 | 8 | 9 | 10 |

Date:     /     / 20

# MOST IMPORTANT TASK OF THE DAY
If you only complete this then today was still a great day

1. _____     ○ ○ ○ ○ ○
                                        HOW WELL I DID

# TASKS OF SECONDARY IMPORTANCE
Getting these done will make my day even greater

2. _____     ○ ○ ○ ○ ○
                                        HOW WELL I DID

3. _____     ○ ○ ○ ○ ○
                                        HOW WELL I DID

# ADDITIONAL TASKS
Don't tackle these until the ones above are done

4. _____     ○ ○ ○ ○ ○
                                        HOW WELL I DID

5. _____     ○ ○ ○ ○ ○
                                        HOW WELL I DID

# NOTES ON MY DAY

_____

_____

_____

## PRODUCTIVITY RATING

1     2     3     4     5     6     7     8     9     10

Date: / / 20

# MOST IMPORTANT TASK OF THE DAY
If you only complete this then today was still a great day

○ ○ ○ ○ ○

1. _____
HOW WELL I DID

# TASKS OF SECONDARY IMPORTANCE
Getting these done will make my day even greater

○ ○ ○ ○ ○

2. _____
HOW WELL I DID

○ ○ ○ ○ ○

3. _____
HOW WELL I DID

# ADDITIONAL TASKS
Don't tackle these until the ones above are done

○ ○ ○ ○ ○

4. _____
HOW WELL I DID

○ ○ ○ ○ ○

5. _____
HOW WELL I DID

# NOTES ON MY DAY

_____

_____

_____

## PRODUCTIVITY RATING

1    2    3    4    5    6    7    8    9    10

Date: / / 20 _____

# MOST IMPORTANT TASK OF THE DAY
If you only complete this then today was still a great day

1. _____   ○○○○○
HOW WELL I DID

# TASKS OF SECONDARY IMPORTANCE
Getting these done will make my day even greater

2. _____   ○○○○○
HOW WELL I DID

3. _____   ○○○○○
HOW WELL I DID

# ADDITIONAL TASKS
Don't tackle these until the ones above are done

4. _____   ○○○○○
HOW WELL I DID

5. _____   ○○○○○
HOW WELL I DID

# NOTES ON MY DAY

_____

_____

_____

## PRODUCTIVITY RATING

1    2    3    4    5    6    7    8    9    10

Date: ___ / ___ / 20_____

# MOST IMPORTANT TASK OF THE DAY
If you only complete this then today was still a great day

1. _____   ○○○○○
HOW WELL I DID

# TASKS OF SECONDARY IMPORTANCE
Getting these done will make my day even greater

2. _____   ○○○○○
HOW WELL I DID

3. _____   ○○○○○
HOW WELL I DID

# ADDITIONAL TASKS
Don't tackle these until the ones above are done

4. _____   ○○○○○
HOW WELL I DID

5. _____   ○○○○○
HOW WELL I DID

# NOTES ON MY DAY

_____

_____

_____

### PRODUCTIVITY RATING

1    2    3    4    5    6    7    8    9    10

# WEEKLY REVIEW

Week of _____

## WEEKLY TRIUMPHS
Want went well this week

_____

_____

_____

## COULD DO BETTER
What fell short of expectations?

_____

_____

_____

## WHAT I'VE LEARNED
Lessons I can grow from

_____

_____

_____

## FOCUS FOR NEXT WEEK
Where I need to spend my energy

_____

_____

Date: ___ / ___ / 20 _____

# MOST IMPORTANT TASK OF THE DAY
If you only complete this then today was still a great day

1. _____  ◯ ◯ ◯ ◯ ◯
HOW WELL I DID

# TASKS OF SECONDARY IMPORTANCE
Getting these done will make my day even greater

2. _____  ◯ ◯ ◯ ◯ ◯
HOW WELL I DID

3. _____  ◯ ◯ ◯ ◯ ◯
HOW WELL I DID

# ADDITIONAL TASKS
Don't tackle these until the ones above are done

4. _____  ◯ ◯ ◯ ◯ ◯
HOW WELL I DID

5. _____  ◯ ◯ ◯ ◯ ◯
HOW WELL I DID

# NOTES ON MY DAY

_____

_____

_____

## PRODUCTIVITY RATING

| 1 | 2 | 3 | 4 | 5 | 6 | 7 | 8 | 9 | 10 |

Date: / / 20

# MOST IMPORTANT TASK OF THE DAY
If you only complete this then today was still a great day

1. _____  ◯ ◯ ◯ ◯ ◯
                              HOW WELL I DID

# TASKS OF SECONDARY IMPORTANCE
Getting these done will make my day even greater

2. _____  ◯ ◯ ◯ ◯ ◯
                              HOW WELL I DID

3. _____  ◯ ◯ ◯ ◯ ◯
                              HOW WELL I DID

# ADDITIONAL TASKS
Don't tackle these until the ones above are done

4. _____  ◯ ◯ ◯ ◯ ◯
                              HOW WELL I DID

5. _____  ◯ ◯ ◯ ◯ ◯
                              HOW WELL I DID

# NOTES ON MY DAY

_____

_____

_____

## PRODUCTIVITY RATING

| 1 | 2 | 3 | 4 | 5 | 6 | 7 | 8 | 9 | 10 |

Date: ___ / ___ / 20 _____

# MOST IMPORTANT TASK OF THE DAY
If you only complete this then today was still a great day

1. _____    ◯◯◯◯◯
                                          HOW WELL I DID

# TASKS OF SECONDARY IMPORTANCE
Getting these done will make my day even greater

2. _____    ◯◯◯◯◯
                                          HOW WELL I DID

3. _____    ◯◯◯◯◯
                                          HOW WELL I DID

# ADDITIONAL TASKS
Don't tackle these until the ones above are done

4. _____    ◯◯◯◯◯
                                          HOW WELL I DID

5. _____    ◯◯◯◯◯
                                          HOW WELL I DID

# NOTES ON MY DAY

_____

_____

_____

## PRODUCTIVITY RATING

1      2      3      4      5      6      7      8      9      10

Date: _____ / _____ / 20 _____

# MOST IMPORTANT TASK OF THE DAY
If you only complete this then today was still a great day

1. _____  ○ ○ ○ ○ ○
                            HOW WELL I DID

# TASKS OF SECONDARY IMPORTANCE
Getting these done will make my day even greater

2. _____  ○ ○ ○ ○ ○
                            HOW WELL I DID

3. _____  ○ ○ ○ ○ ○
                            HOW WELL I DID

# ADDITIONAL TASKS
Don't tackle these until the ones above are done

4. _____  ○ ○ ○ ○ ○
                            HOW WELL I DID

5. _____  ○ ○ ○ ○ ○
                            HOW WELL I DID

# NOTES ON MY DAY

_____

_____

_____

## PRODUCTIVITY RATING

1    2    3    4    5    6    7    8    9    10

Date: __/__/ 20____

# MOST IMPORTANT TASK OF THE DAY
If you only complete this then today was still a great day

1. _____  ◯ ◯ ◯ ◯ ◯
HOW WELL I DID

# TASKS OF SECONDARY IMPORTANCE
Getting these done will make my day even greater

2. _____  ◯ ◯ ◯ ◯ ◯
HOW WELL I DID

3. _____  ◯ ◯ ◯ ◯ ◯
HOW WELL I DID

# ADDITIONAL TASKS
Don't tackle these until the ones above are done

4. _____  ◯ ◯ ◯ ◯ ◯
HOW WELL I DID

5. _____  ◯ ◯ ◯ ◯ ◯
HOW WELL I DID

# NOTES ON MY DAY

_____

_____

_____

## PRODUCTIVITY RATING

1    2    3    4    5    6    7    8    9    10

# WEEKLY REVIEW

Week of _____

## WEEKLY TRIUMPHS
Want went well this week

_____

_____

_____

## COULD DO BETTER
What fell short of expectations?

_____

_____

_____

## WHAT I'VE LEARNED
Lessons I can grow from

_____

_____

_____

## FOCUS FOR NEXT WEEK
Where I need to spend my energy

_____

_____

Date: __ / __ / 20 ____

# MOST IMPORTANT TASK OF THE DAY
If you only complete this then today was still a great day

1. _____  ◯ ◯ ◯ ◯ ◯
HOW WELL I DID

# TASKS OF SECONDARY IMPORTANCE
Getting these done will make my day even greater

2. _____  ◯ ◯ ◯ ◯ ◯
HOW WELL I DID

3. _____  ◯ ◯ ◯ ◯ ◯
HOW WELL I DID

# ADDITIONAL TASKS
Don't tackle these until the ones above are done

4. _____  ◯ ◯ ◯ ◯ ◯
HOW WELL I DID

5. _____  ◯ ◯ ◯ ◯ ◯
HOW WELL I DID

# NOTES ON MY DAY

_____

_____

_____

## PRODUCTIVITY RATING

| 1 | 2 | 3 | 4 | 5 | 6 | 7 | 8 | 9 | 10 |

Date:  /  / 20

# MOST IMPORTANT TASK OF THE DAY
If you only complete this then today was still a great day

1. _____     ○ ○ ○ ○ ○
HOW WELL I DID

# TASKS OF SECONDARY IMPORTANCE
Getting these done will make my day even greater

2. _____     ○ ○ ○ ○ ○
HOW WELL I DID

3. _____     ○ ○ ○ ○ ○
HOW WELL I DID

# ADDITIONAL TASKS
Don't tackle these until the ones above are done

4. _____     ○ ○ ○ ○ ○
HOW WELL I DID

5. _____     ○ ○ ○ ○ ○
HOW WELL I DID

# NOTES ON MY DAY

_____

_____

_____

**PRODUCTIVITY RATING**

1    2    3    4    5    6    7    8    9    10

Date: __ / __ / 20____

# MOST IMPORTANT TASK OF THE DAY
If you only complete this then today was still a great day

1. _____  ○ ○ ○ ○ ○
HOW WELL I DID

# TASKS OF SECONDARY IMPORTANCE
Getting these done will make my day even greater

2. _____  ○ ○ ○ ○ ○
HOW WELL I DID

3. _____  ○ ○ ○ ○ ○
HOW WELL I DID

# ADDITIONAL TASKS
Don't tackle these until the ones above are done

4. _____  ○ ○ ○ ○ ○
HOW WELL I DID

5. _____  ○ ○ ○ ○ ○
HOW WELL I DID

# NOTES ON MY DAY

_____

_____

_____

## PRODUCTIVITY RATING

1    2    3    4    5    6    7    8    9    10

Date: ___ / ___ / 20 ___

# MOST IMPORTANT TASK OF THE DAY
If you only complete this then today was still a great day

1. _____  ○ ○ ○ ○ ○
HOW WELL I DID

# TASKS OF SECONDARY IMPORTANCE
Getting these done will make my day even greater

2. _____  ○ ○ ○ ○ ○
HOW WELL I DID

3. _____  ○ ○ ○ ○ ○
HOW WELL I DID

# ADDITIONAL TASKS
Don't tackle these until the ones above are done

4. _____  ○ ○ ○ ○ ○
HOW WELL I DID

5. _____  ○ ○ ○ ○ ○
HOW WELL I DID

# NOTES ON MY DAY

_____

_____

_____

## PRODUCTIVITY RATING

| 1 | 2 | 3 | 4 | 5 | 6 | 7 | 8 | 9 | 10 |

Date:  /  / 20 _____

# MOST IMPORTANT TASK OF THE DAY

If you only complete this then today was still a great day

1. _____  ◯ ◯ ◯ ◯ ◯
HOW WELL I DID

# TASKS OF SECONDARY IMPORTANCE

Getting these done will make my day even greater

2. _____  ◯ ◯ ◯ ◯ ◯
HOW WELL I DID

3. _____  ◯ ◯ ◯ ◯ ◯
HOW WELL I DID

# ADDITIONAL TASKS

Don't tackle these until the ones above are done

4. _____  ◯ ◯ ◯ ◯ ◯
HOW WELL I DID

5. _____  ◯ ◯ ◯ ◯ ◯
HOW WELL I DID

# NOTES ON MY DAY

_____

_____

_____

### PRODUCTIVITY RATING

1    2    3    4    5    6    7    8    9    10

# WEEKLY REVIEW

Week of _____

## WEEKLY TRIUMPHS
Want went well this week

_____

_____

_____

## COULD DO BETTER
What fell short of expectations?

_____

_____

_____

## WHAT I'VE LEARNED
Lessons I can grow from

_____

_____

_____

## FOCUS FOR NEXT WEEK
Where I need to spend my energy

_____

_____

Date: ___ / ___ / 20_____

# MOST IMPORTANT TASK OF THE DAY
If you only complete this then today was still a great day

1. _____  ○ ○ ○ ○ ○
HOW WELL I DID

# TASKS OF SECONDARY IMPORTANCE
Getting these done will make my day even greater

2. _____  ○ ○ ○ ○ ○
HOW WELL I DID

3. _____  ○ ○ ○ ○ ○
HOW WELL I DID

# ADDITIONAL TASKS
Don't tackle these until the ones above are done

4. _____  ○ ○ ○ ○ ○
HOW WELL I DID

5. _____  ○ ○ ○ ○ ○
HOW WELL I DID

# NOTES ON MY DAY

_____

_____

_____

**PRODUCTIVITY RATING**

1    2    3    4    5    6    7    8    9    10

Date:    /    / 20 _____

# MOST IMPORTANT TASK OF THE DAY
If you only complete this then today was still a great day

1. _____  ○ ○ ○ ○ ○
HOW WELL I DID

# TASKS OF SECONDARY IMPORTANCE
Getting these done will make my day even greater

2. _____  ○ ○ ○ ○ ○
HOW WELL I DID

3. _____  ○ ○ ○ ○ ○
HOW WELL I DID

# ADDITIONAL TASKS
Don't tackle these until the ones above are done

4. _____  ○ ○ ○ ○ ○
HOW WELL I DID

5. _____  ○ ○ ○ ○ ○
HOW WELL I DID

# NOTES ON MY DAY

_____

_____

_____

## PRODUCTIVITY RATING

1    2    3    4    5    6    7    8    9    10

Date: / / 20 _____

# MOST IMPORTANT TASK OF THE DAY
If you only complete this then today was still a great day

1. _____ ○ ○ ○ ○ ○
HOW WELL I DID

# TASKS OF SECONDARY IMPORTANCE
Getting these done will make my day even greater

2. _____ ○ ○ ○ ○ ○
HOW WELL I DID

3. _____ ○ ○ ○ ○ ○
HOW WELL I DID

# ADDITIONAL TASKS
Don't tackle these until the ones above are done

4. _____ ○ ○ ○ ○ ○
HOW WELL I DID

5. _____ ○ ○ ○ ○ ○
HOW WELL I DID

# NOTES ON MY DAY

_____

_____

_____

**PRODUCTIVITY RATING**

1　　2　　3　　4　　5　　6　　7　　8　　9　　10

Date: ___/___/ 20___

# MOST IMPORTANT TASK OF THE DAY
If you only complete this then today was still a great day

1. _____  ○ ○ ○ ○ ○
HOW WELL I DID

# TASKS OF SECONDARY IMPORTANCE
Getting these done will make my day even greater

2. _____  ○ ○ ○ ○ ○
HOW WELL I DID

3. _____  ○ ○ ○ ○ ○
HOW WELL I DID

# ADDITIONAL TASKS
Don't tackle these until the ones above are done

4. _____  ○ ○ ○ ○ ○
HOW WELL I DID

5. _____  ○ ○ ○ ○ ○
HOW WELL I DID

# NOTES ON MY DAY

_____

_____

_____

**PRODUCTIVITY RATING**

1    2    3    4    5    6    7    8    9    10

Date:  /  / 20 _____

# MOST IMPORTANT TASK OF THE DAY
If you only complete this then today was still a great day

1. _____  ○ ○ ○ ○ ○
HOW WELL I DID

# TASKS OF SECONDARY IMPORTANCE
Getting these done will make my day even greater

2. _____  ○ ○ ○ ○ ○
HOW WELL I DID

3. _____  ○ ○ ○ ○ ○
HOW WELL I DID

# ADDITIONAL TASKS
Don't tackle these until the ones above are done

4. _____  ○ ○ ○ ○ ○
HOW WELL I DID

5. _____  ○ ○ ○ ○ ○
HOW WELL I DID

# NOTES ON MY DAY

_____

_____

_____

## PRODUCTIVITY RATING

1    2    3    4    5    6    7    8    9    10

# WEEKLY REVIEW

Week of _____

## WEEKLY TRIUMPHS
Want went well this week

_____

_____

_____

## COULD DO BETTER
What fell short of expectations?

_____

_____

_____

## WHAT I'VE LEARNED
Lessons I can grow from

_____

_____

_____

## FOCUS FOR NEXT WEEK
Where I need to spend my energy

_____

_____

Date: ___ / ___ / 20 _____

# MOST IMPORTANT TASK OF THE DAY
If you only complete this then today was still a great day

1. _____ ○○○○○
HOW WELL I DID

# TASKS OF SECONDARY IMPORTANCE
Getting these done will make my day even greater

2. _____ ○○○○○
HOW WELL I DID

3. _____ ○○○○○
HOW WELL I DID

# ADDITIONAL TASKS
Don't tackle these until the ones above are done

4. _____ ○○○○○
HOW WELL I DID

5. _____ ○○○○○
HOW WELL I DID

# NOTES ON MY DAY

_____

_____

_____

**PRODUCTIVITY RATING**

| 1 | 2 | 3 | 4 | 5 | 6 | 7 | 8 | 9 | 10 |

Date:     /     / 20 _____

# MOST IMPORTANT TASK OF THE DAY
If you only complete this then today was still a great day

1. _____  ◯ ◯ ◯ ◯ ◯
HOW WELL I DID

# TASKS OF SECONDARY IMPORTANCE
Getting these done will make my day even greater

2. _____  ◯ ◯ ◯ ◯ ◯
HOW WELL I DID

3. _____  ◯ ◯ ◯ ◯ ◯
HOW WELL I DID

# ADDITIONAL TASKS
Don't tackle these until the ones above are done

4. _____  ◯ ◯ ◯ ◯ ◯
HOW WELL I DID

5. _____  ◯ ◯ ◯ ◯ ◯
HOW WELL I DID

# NOTES ON MY DAY

_____

_____

_____

## PRODUCTIVITY RATING

1      2      3      4      5      6      7      8      9      10

Date: / / 20

# MOST IMPORTANT TASK OF THE DAY
If you only complete this then today was still a great day

1. _____   ◯◯◯◯◯
HOW WELL I DID

# TASKS OF SECONDARY IMPORTANCE
Getting these done will make my day even greater

2. _____   ◯◯◯◯◯
HOW WELL I DID

3. _____   ◯◯◯◯◯
HOW WELL I DID

# ADDITIONAL TASKS
Don't tackle these until the ones above are done

4. _____   ◯◯◯◯◯
HOW WELL I DID

5. _____   ◯◯◯◯◯
HOW WELL I DID

# NOTES ON MY DAY

_____

_____

_____

## PRODUCTIVITY RATING

1    2    3    4    5    6    7    8    9    10

Date: / / 20 _____

# MOST IMPORTANT TASK OF THE DAY
If you only complete this then today was still a great day

1. _____  ○ ○ ○ ○ ○
HOW WELL I DID

# TASKS OF SECONDARY IMPORTANCE
Getting these done will make my day even greater

2. _____  ○ ○ ○ ○ ○
HOW WELL I DID

3. _____  ○ ○ ○ ○ ○
HOW WELL I DID

# ADDITIONAL TASKS
Don't tackle these until the ones above are done

4. _____  ○ ○ ○ ○ ○
HOW WELL I DID

5. _____  ○ ○ ○ ○ ○
HOW WELL I DID

# NOTES ON MY DAY

_____

_____

_____

## PRODUCTIVITY RATING

1    2    3    4    5    6    7    8    9    10

Date:    /    / 20 _____

# MOST IMPORTANT TASK OF THE DAY
If you only complete this then today was still a great day

○ ○ ○ ○ ○

1. _____
HOW WELL I DID

# TASKS OF SECONDARY IMPORTANCE
Getting these done will make my day even greater

○ ○ ○ ○ ○

2. _____
HOW WELL I DID

○ ○ ○ ○ ○

3. _____
HOW WELL I DID

# ADDITIONAL TASKS
Don't tackle these until the ones above are done

○ ○ ○ ○ ○

4. _____
HOW WELL I DID

○ ○ ○ ○ ○

5. _____
HOW WELL I DID

# NOTES ON MY DAY

_____

_____

_____

**PRODUCTIVITY RATING**

1    2    3    4    5    6    7    8    9    10

# WEEKLY REVIEW

Week of _____

## WEEKLY TRIUMPHS
Want went well this week

_____

_____

_____

## COULD DO BETTER
What fell short of expectations?

_____

_____

_____

## WHAT I'VE LEARNED
Lessons I can grow from

_____

_____

_____

## FOCUS FOR NEXT WEEK
Where I need to spend my energy

_____

_____

Date: _/_/ 20_

# MOST IMPORTANT TASK OF THE DAY
If you only complete this then today was still a great day

1. _____  ◯◯◯◯◯
HOW WELL I DID

# TASKS OF SECONDARY IMPORTANCE
Getting these done will make my day even greater

2. _____  ◯◯◯◯◯
HOW WELL I DID

3. _____  ◯◯◯◯◯
HOW WELL I DID

# ADDITIONAL TASKS
Don't tackle these until the ones above are done

4. _____  ◯◯◯◯◯
HOW WELL I DID

5. _____  ◯◯◯◯◯
HOW WELL I DID

# NOTES ON MY DAY

_____

_____

_____

## PRODUCTIVITY RATING

1    2    3    4    5    6    7    8    9    10

Date: ___ / ___ / 20 ___

# MOST IMPORTANT TASK OF THE DAY
If you only complete this then today was still a great day

1. _____    ◯ ◯ ◯ ◯ ◯
HOW WELL I DID

# TASKS OF SECONDARY IMPORTANCE
Getting these done will make my day even greater

2. _____    ◯ ◯ ◯ ◯ ◯
HOW WELL I DID

3. _____    ◯ ◯ ◯ ◯ ◯
HOW WELL I DID

# ADDITIONAL TASKS
Don't tackle these until the ones above are done

4. _____    ◯ ◯ ◯ ◯ ◯
HOW WELL I DID

5. _____    ◯ ◯ ◯ ◯ ◯
HOW WELL I DID

# NOTES ON MY DAY

_____

_____

_____

## PRODUCTIVITY RATING

1     2     3     4     5     6     7     8     9     10

Date:  /  / 20 _____

# MOST IMPORTANT TASK OF THE DAY
If you only complete this then today was still a great day

1. _____   ◯ ◯ ◯ ◯ ◯
HOW WELL I DID

# TASKS OF SECONDARY IMPORTANCE
Getting these done will make my day even greater

2. _____   ◯ ◯ ◯ ◯ ◯
HOW WELL I DID

3. _____   ◯ ◯ ◯ ◯ ◯
HOW WELL I DID

# ADDITIONAL TASKS
Don't tackle these until the ones above are done

4. _____   ◯ ◯ ◯ ◯ ◯
HOW WELL I DID

5. _____   ◯ ◯ ◯ ◯ ◯
HOW WELL I DID

# NOTES ON MY DAY

_____

_____

_____

**PRODUCTIVITY RATING**

1     2     3     4     5     6     7     8     9     10

Date:  /  / 20

# MOST IMPORTANT TASK OF THE DAY
If you only complete this then today was still a great day

1. _____  ○ ○ ○ ○ ○
HOW WELL I DID

# TASKS OF SECONDARY IMPORTANCE
Getting these done will make my day even greater

2. _____  ○ ○ ○ ○ ○
HOW WELL I DID

3. _____  ○ ○ ○ ○ ○
HOW WELL I DID

# ADDITIONAL TASKS
Don't tackle these until the ones above are done

4. _____  ○ ○ ○ ○ ○
HOW WELL I DID

5. _____  ○ ○ ○ ○ ○
HOW WELL I DID

# NOTES ON MY DAY

_____

_____

_____

## PRODUCTIVITY RATING

1    2    3    4    5    6    7    8    9    10

Date: ___ / ___ / 20 _____

# MOST IMPORTANT TASK OF THE DAY
If you only complete this then today was still a great day

1. _____  ◯◯◯◯◯
HOW WELL I DID

# TASKS OF SECONDARY IMPORTANCE
Getting these done will make my day even greater

2. _____  ◯◯◯◯◯
HOW WELL I DID

3. _____  ◯◯◯◯◯
HOW WELL I DID

# ADDITIONAL TASKS
Don't tackle these until the ones above are done

4. _____  ◯◯◯◯◯
HOW WELL I DID

5. _____  ◯◯◯◯◯
HOW WELL I DID

# NOTES ON MY DAY

_____

_____

_____

### PRODUCTIVITY RATING

1    2    3    4    5    6    7    8    9    10

# WEEKLY REVIEW

Week of _____

## WEEKLY TRIUMPHS
Want went well this week

_____

_____

_____

## COULD DO BETTER
What fell short of expectations?

_____

_____

_____

## WHAT I'VE LEARNED
Lessons I can grow from

_____

_____

_____

## FOCUS FOR NEXT WEEK
Where I need to spend my energy

_____

_____

Date: __/__/ 20_____

# MOST IMPORTANT TASK OF THE DAY
If you only complete this then today was still a great day

1. _____ ○○○○○
HOW WELL I DID

# TASKS OF SECONDARY IMPORTANCE
Getting these done will make my day even greater

2. _____ ○○○○○
HOW WELL I DID

3. _____ ○○○○○
HOW WELL I DID

# ADDITIONAL TASKS
Don't tackle these until the ones above are done

4. _____ ○○○○○
HOW WELL I DID

5. _____ ○○○○○
HOW WELL I DID

# NOTES ON MY DAY

_____

_____

_____

## PRODUCTIVITY RATING

1        2        3        4        5        6        7        8        9        10

Date:    /    / 20 _____

# MOST IMPORTANT TASK OF THE DAY
If you only complete this then today was still a great day

1. _____    ◯ ◯ ◯ ◯ ◯
                                 HOW WELL I DID

# TASKS OF SECONDARY IMPORTANCE
Getting these done will make my day even greater

2. _____    ◯ ◯ ◯ ◯ ◯
                                 HOW WELL I DID

3. _____    ◯ ◯ ◯ ◯ ◯
                                 HOW WELL I DID

# ADDITIONAL TASKS
Don't tackle these until the ones above are done

4. _____    ◯ ◯ ◯ ◯ ◯
                                 HOW WELL I DID

5. _____    ◯ ◯ ◯ ◯ ◯
                                 HOW WELL I DID

# NOTES ON MY DAY

_____

_____

_____

## PRODUCTIVITY RATING

1    2    3    4    5    6    7    8    9    10

Date:  /  / 20 _____

# MOST IMPORTANT TASK OF THE DAY
If you only complete this then today was still a great day

○ ○ ○ ○ ○

1. _____     HOW WELL I DID

# TASKS OF SECONDARY IMPORTANCE
Getting these done will make my day even greater

○ ○ ○ ○ ○

2. _____     HOW WELL I DID

○ ○ ○ ○ ○

3. _____     HOW WELL I DID

# ADDITIONAL TASKS
Don't tackle these until the ones above are done

○ ○ ○ ○ ○

4. _____     HOW WELL I DID

○ ○ ○ ○ ○

5. _____     HOW WELL I DID

# NOTES ON MY DAY

_____

_____

_____

## PRODUCTIVITY RATING

1    2    3    4    5    6    7    8    9    10

Date:  /   / 20 _____

# MOST IMPORTANT TASK OF THE DAY
If you only complete this then today was still a great day

○ ○ ○ ○ ○

1. _____
HOW WELL I DID

# TASKS OF SECONDARY IMPORTANCE
Getting these done will make my day even greater

○ ○ ○ ○ ○

2. _____
HOW WELL I DID

○ ○ ○ ○ ○

3. _____
HOW WELL I DID

# ADDITIONAL TASKS
Don't tackle these until the ones above are done

○ ○ ○ ○ ○

4. _____
HOW WELL I DID

○ ○ ○ ○ ○

5. _____
HOW WELL I DID

# NOTES ON MY DAY

_____

_____

_____

## PRODUCTIVITY RATING

1    2    3    4    5    6    7    8    9    10

Date: / / 20 _____

# MOST IMPORTANT TASK OF THE DAY
If you only complete this then today was still a great day

1. _____  ◯ ◯ ◯ ◯ ◯
HOW WELL I DID

# TASKS OF SECONDARY IMPORTANCE
Getting these done will make my day even greater

2. _____  ◯ ◯ ◯ ◯ ◯
HOW WELL I DID

3. _____  ◯ ◯ ◯ ◯ ◯
HOW WELL I DID

# ADDITIONAL TASKS
Don't tackle these until the ones above are done

4. _____  ◯ ◯ ◯ ◯ ◯
HOW WELL I DID

5. _____  ◯ ◯ ◯ ◯ ◯
HOW WELL I DID

# NOTES ON MY DAY

_____

_____

_____

## PRODUCTIVITY RATING

1     2     3     4     5     6     7     8     9     10

# WEEKLY REVIEW

Week of _____

## WEEKLY TRIUMPHS
Want went well this week

_____

_____

_____

## COULD DO BETTER
What fell short of expectations?

_____

_____

_____

## WHAT I'VE LEARNED
Lessons I can grow from

_____

_____

_____

## FOCUS FOR NEXT WEEK
Where I need to spend my energy

_____

_____

Date: / / 20

# MOST IMPORTANT TASK OF THE DAY
If you only complete this then today was still a great day

○○○○○

1. _____
HOW WELL I DID

# TASKS OF SECONDARY IMPORTANCE
Getting these done will make my day even greater

○○○○○

2. _____
HOW WELL I DID

○○○○○

3. _____
HOW WELL I DID

# ADDITIONAL TASKS
Don't tackle these until the ones above are done

○○○○○

4. _____
HOW WELL I DID

○○○○○

5. _____
HOW WELL I DID

# NOTES ON MY DAY

_____

_____

_____

### PRODUCTIVITY RATING

| 1 | 2 | 3 | 4 | 5 | 6 | 7 | 8 | 9 | 10 |

Date:  /  / 20

# MOST IMPORTANT TASK OF THE DAY
If you only complete this then today was still a great day

1. _____  ◯ ◯ ◯ ◯ ◯
HOW WELL I DID

# TASKS OF SECONDARY IMPORTANCE
Getting these done will make my day even greater

2. _____  ◯ ◯ ◯ ◯ ◯
HOW WELL I DID

3. _____  ◯ ◯ ◯ ◯ ◯
HOW WELL I DID

# ADDITIONAL TASKS
Don't tackle these until the ones above are done

4. _____  ◯ ◯ ◯ ◯ ◯
HOW WELL I DID

5. _____  ◯ ◯ ◯ ◯ ◯
HOW WELL I DID

# NOTES ON MY DAY

_____

_____

_____

## PRODUCTIVITY RATING

| 1 | 2 | 3 | 4 | 5 | 6 | 7 | 8 | 9 | 10 |

Date: ___ / ___ / 20 _____

# MOST IMPORTANT TASK OF THE DAY
If you only complete this then today was still a great day

1. _____ ○○○○○
HOW WELL I DID

# TASKS OF SECONDARY IMPORTANCE
Getting these done will make my day even greater

2. _____ ○○○○○
HOW WELL I DID

3. _____ ○○○○○
HOW WELL I DID

# ADDITIONAL TASKS
Don't tackle these until the ones above are done

4. _____ ○○○○○
HOW WELL I DID

5. _____ ○○○○○
HOW WELL I DID

# NOTES ON MY DAY

_____

_____

_____

## PRODUCTIVITY RATING

| 1 | 2 | 3 | 4 | 5 | 6 | 7 | 8 | 9 | 10 |

Date: ___/___/20_____

# MOST IMPORTANT TASK OF THE DAY
If you only complete this then today was still a great day

1. _____  ○ ○ ○ ○ ○
HOW WELL I DID

# TASKS OF SECONDARY IMPORTANCE
Getting these done will make my day even greater

2. _____  ○ ○ ○ ○ ○
HOW WELL I DID

3. _____  ○ ○ ○ ○ ○
HOW WELL I DID

# ADDITIONAL TASKS
Don't tackle these until the ones above are done

4. _____  ○ ○ ○ ○ ○
HOW WELL I DID

5. _____  ○ ○ ○ ○ ○
HOW WELL I DID

# NOTES ON MY DAY

_____

_____

_____

## PRODUCTIVITY RATING

1    2    3    4    5    6    7    8    9    10

Date:  /  / 20 _____

# MOST IMPORTANT TASK OF THE DAY
If you only complete this then today was still a great day

○ ○ ○ ○ ○

1. _____

HOW WELL I DID

# TASKS OF SECONDARY IMPORTANCE
Getting these done will make my day even greater

○ ○ ○ ○ ○

2. _____

HOW WELL I DID

○ ○ ○ ○ ○

3. _____

HOW WELL I DID

# ADDITIONAL TASKS
Don't tackle these until the ones above are done

○ ○ ○ ○ ○

4. _____

HOW WELL I DID

○ ○ ○ ○ ○

5. _____

HOW WELL I DID

# NOTES ON MY DAY

_____

_____

_____

### PRODUCTIVITY RATING

| 1 | 2 | 3 | 4 | 5 | 6 | 7 | 8 | 9 | 10 |

# WEEKLY REVIEW

Week of _____

## WEEKLY TRIUMPHS
Want went well this week

_____

_____

_____

## COULD DO BETTER
What fell short of expectations?

_____

_____

_____

## WHAT I'VE LEARNED
Lessons I can grow from

_____

_____

_____

## FOCUS FOR NEXT WEEK
Where I need to spend my energy

_____

_____

Date: ___ / ___ / 20 _____

# MOST IMPORTANT TASK OF THE DAY
If you only complete this then today was still a great day

1. _____  ○ ○ ○ ○ ○
HOW WELL I DID

# TASKS OF SECONDARY IMPORTANCE
Getting these done will make my day even greater

2. _____  ○ ○ ○ ○ ○
HOW WELL I DID

3. _____  ○ ○ ○ ○ ○
HOW WELL I DID

# ADDITIONAL TASKS
Don't tackle these until the ones above are done

4. _____  ○ ○ ○ ○ ○
HOW WELL I DID

5. _____  ○ ○ ○ ○ ○
HOW WELL I DID

# NOTES ON MY DAY

_____

_____

_____

## PRODUCTIVITY RATING

1    2    3    4    5    6    7    8    9    10

Date: ___/___/20 ____

# MOST IMPORTANT TASK OF THE DAY

If you only complete this then today was still a great day

1. _____    ○ ○ ○ ○ ○
                                  HOW WELL I DID

# TASKS OF SECONDARY IMPORTANCE

Getting these done will make my day even greater

2. _____    ○ ○ ○ ○ ○
                                  HOW WELL I DID

3. _____    ○ ○ ○ ○ ○
                                  HOW WELL I DID

# ADDITIONAL TASKS

Don't tackle these until the ones above are done

4. _____    ○ ○ ○ ○ ○
                                  HOW WELL I DID

5. _____    ○ ○ ○ ○ ○
                                  HOW WELL I DID

# NOTES ON MY DAY

_____

_____

_____

### PRODUCTIVITY RATING

1    2    3    4    5    6    7    8    9    10

Date: ___/___/ 20_____

# MOST IMPORTANT TASK OF THE DAY
If you only complete this then today was still a great day

1. _____    ○○○○○
HOW WELL I DID

# TASKS OF SECONDARY IMPORTANCE
Getting these done will make my day even greater

2. _____    ○○○○○
HOW WELL I DID

3. _____    ○○○○○
HOW WELL I DID

# ADDITIONAL TASKS
Don't tackle these until the ones above are done

4. _____    ○○○○○
HOW WELL I DID

5. _____    ○○○○○
HOW WELL I DID

# NOTES ON MY DAY

_____

_____

_____

## PRODUCTIVITY RATING

1    2    3    4    5    6    7    8    9    10

Date:  /  / 20 _____

# MOST IMPORTANT TASK OF THE DAY
If you only complete this then today was still a great day

1. _____  ○○○○○
HOW WELL I DID

# TASKS OF SECONDARY IMPORTANCE
Getting these done will make my day even greater

2. _____  ○○○○○
HOW WELL I DID

3. _____  ○○○○○
HOW WELL I DID

# ADDITIONAL TASKS
Don't tackle these until the ones above are done

4. _____  ○○○○○
HOW WELL I DID

5. _____  ○○○○○
HOW WELL I DID

# NOTES ON MY DAY

_____

_____

_____

## PRODUCTIVITY RATING

| 1 | 2 | 3 | 4 | 5 | 6 | 7 | 8 | 9 | 10 |

Date: ___/___/ 20_____

# MOST IMPORTANT TASK OF THE DAY
If you only complete this then today was still a great day

1. _____   ○ ○ ○ ○ ○
HOW WELL I DID

# TASKS OF SECONDARY IMPORTANCE
Getting these done will make my day even greater

2. _____   ○ ○ ○ ○ ○
HOW WELL I DID

3. _____   ○ ○ ○ ○ ○
HOW WELL I DID

# ADDITIONAL TASKS
Don't tackle these until the ones above are done

4. _____   ○ ○ ○ ○ ○
HOW WELL I DID

5. _____   ○ ○ ○ ○ ○
HOW WELL I DID

# NOTES ON MY DAY

_____

_____

_____

## PRODUCTIVITY RATING

1    2    3    4    5    6    7    8    9    10

# WEEKLY REVIEW

Week of _____

## WEEKLY TRIUMPHS
Want went well this week

_____

_____

_____

## COULD DO BETTER
What fell short of expectations?

_____

_____

_____

## WHAT I'VE LEARNED
Lessons I can grow from

_____

_____

_____

## FOCUS FOR NEXT WEEK
Where I need to spend my energy

_____

_____

Date: ___ / ___ / 20 _____

# MOST IMPORTANT TASK OF THE DAY
If you only complete this then today was still a great day

○ ○ ○ ○ ○

1. _____
HOW WELL I DID

# TASKS OF SECONDARY IMPORTANCE
Getting these done will make my day even greater

○ ○ ○ ○ ○

2. _____
HOW WELL I DID

○ ○ ○ ○ ○

3. _____
HOW WELL I DID

# ADDITIONAL TASKS
Don't tackle these until the ones above are done

○ ○ ○ ○ ○

4. _____
HOW WELL I DID

○ ○ ○ ○ ○

5. _____
HOW WELL I DID

# NOTES ON MY DAY

_____

_____

_____

**PRODUCTIVITY RATING**

1     2     3     4     5     6     7     8     9     10

Date:  /  / 20 _____

# MOST IMPORTANT TASK OF THE DAY
If you only complete this then today was still a great day

1. _____
HOW WELL I DID

# TASKS OF SECONDARY IMPORTANCE
Getting these done will make my day even greater

2. _____
HOW WELL I DID

3. _____
HOW WELL I DID

# ADDITIONAL TASKS
Don't tackle these until the ones above are done

4. _____
HOW WELL I DID

5. _____
HOW WELL I DID

# NOTES ON MY DAY

_____

_____

_____

**PRODUCTIVITY RATING**

1    2    3    4    5    6    7    8    9    10

Date:     /     / 20 _____

# MOST IMPORTANT TASK OF THE DAY
If you only complete this then today was still a great day

1. _____     ○ ○ ○ ○ ○
                                          HOW WELL I DID

# TASKS OF SECONDARY IMPORTANCE
Getting these done will make my day even greater

2. _____     ○ ○ ○ ○ ○
                                          HOW WELL I DID

3. _____     ○ ○ ○ ○ ○
                                          HOW WELL I DID

# ADDITIONAL TASKS
Don't tackle these until the ones above are done

4. _____     ○ ○ ○ ○ ○
                                          HOW WELL I DID

5. _____     ○ ○ ○ ○ ○
                                          HOW WELL I DID

# NOTES ON MY DAY

_____

_____

_____

## PRODUCTIVITY RATING

1     2     3     4     5     6     7     8     9     10

Date: ___ / ___ / 20 _____

# MOST IMPORTANT TASK OF THE DAY
If you only complete this then today was still a great day

1. _____   ○ ○ ○ ○ ○
HOW WELL I DID

# TASKS OF SECONDARY IMPORTANCE
Getting these done will make my day even greater

2. _____   ○ ○ ○ ○ ○
HOW WELL I DID

3. _____   ○ ○ ○ ○ ○
HOW WELL I DID

# ADDITIONAL TASKS
Don't tackle these until the ones above are done

4. _____   ○ ○ ○ ○ ○
HOW WELL I DID

5. _____   ○ ○ ○ ○ ○
HOW WELL I DID

# NOTES ON MY DAY

_____

_____

_____

## PRODUCTIVITY RATING

| 1 | 2 | 3 | 4 | 5 | 6 | 7 | 8 | 9 | 10 |

Date:  /  / 20 _____

# MOST IMPORTANT TASK OF THE DAY
If you only complete this then today was still a great day

1. _____  ○○○○○
HOW WELL I DID

# TASKS OF SECONDARY IMPORTANCE
Getting these done will make my day even greater

2. _____  ○○○○○
HOW WELL I DID

3. _____  ○○○○○
HOW WELL I DID

# ADDITIONAL TASKS
Don't tackle these until the ones above are done

4. _____  ○○○○○
HOW WELL I DID

5. _____  ○○○○○
HOW WELL I DID

# NOTES ON MY DAY

_____

_____

_____

## PRODUCTIVITY RATING

| 1 | 2 | 3 | 4 | 5 | 6 | 7 | 8 | 9 | 10 |

# WEEKLY REVIEW

Week of _____

## WEEKLY TRIUMPHS
Want went well this week

_____

_____

_____

## COULD DO BETTER
What fell short of expectations?

_____

_____

_____

## WHAT I'VE LEARNED
Lessons I can grow from

_____

_____

_____

## FOCUS FOR NEXT WEEK
Where I need to spend my energy

_____

_____

Date:  /  / 20 _____

# MOST IMPORTANT TASK OF THE DAY
If you only complete this then today was still a great day

○ ○ ○ ○ ○

1. _____
HOW WELL I DID

# TASKS OF SECONDARY IMPORTANCE
Getting these done will make my day even greater

○ ○ ○ ○ ○

2. _____
HOW WELL I DID

○ ○ ○ ○ ○

3. _____
HOW WELL I DID

# ADDITIONAL TASKS
Don't tackle these until the ones above are done

○ ○ ○ ○ ○

4. _____
HOW WELL I DID

○ ○ ○ ○ ○

5. _____
HOW WELL I DID

# NOTES ON MY DAY

_____

_____

_____

## PRODUCTIVITY RATING

1    2    3    4    5    6    7    8    9    10

Date:  /  / 20 _____

# MOST IMPORTANT TASK OF THE DAY
If you only complete this then today was still a great day

1. _____  ○ ○ ○ ○ ○
HOW WELL I DID

# TASKS OF SECONDARY IMPORTANCE
Getting these done will make my day even greater

2. _____  ○ ○ ○ ○ ○
HOW WELL I DID

3. _____  ○ ○ ○ ○ ○
HOW WELL I DID

# ADDITIONAL TASKS
Don't tackle these until the ones above are done

4. _____  ○ ○ ○ ○ ○
HOW WELL I DID

5. _____  ○ ○ ○ ○ ○
HOW WELL I DID

# NOTES ON MY DAY

_____

_____

_____

## PRODUCTIVITY RATING
1    2    3    4    5    6    7    8    9    10

Date:  /  / 20 _____

# MOST IMPORTANT TASK OF THE DAY
If you only complete this then today was still a great day

1. _____  ○ ○ ○ ○ ○
HOW WELL I DID

# TASKS OF SECONDARY IMPORTANCE
Getting these done will make my day even greater

2. _____  ○ ○ ○ ○ ○
HOW WELL I DID

3. _____  ○ ○ ○ ○ ○
HOW WELL I DID

# ADDITIONAL TASKS
Don't tackle these until the ones above are done

4. _____  ○ ○ ○ ○ ○
HOW WELL I DID

5. _____  ○ ○ ○ ○ ○
HOW WELL I DID

# NOTES ON MY DAY

_____

_____

_____

## PRODUCTIVITY RATING

1    2    3    4    5    6    7    8    9    10

Date: ___/___/ 20_____

# MOST IMPORTANT TASK OF THE DAY
If you only complete this then today was still a great day

1. _____  ◯ ◯ ◯ ◯ ◯
HOW WELL I DID

# TASKS OF SECONDARY IMPORTANCE
Getting these done will make my day even greater

2. _____  ◯ ◯ ◯ ◯ ◯
HOW WELL I DID

3. _____  ◯ ◯ ◯ ◯ ◯
HOW WELL I DID

# ADDITIONAL TASKS
Don't tackle these until the ones above are done

4. _____  ◯ ◯ ◯ ◯ ◯
HOW WELL I DID

5. _____  ◯ ◯ ◯ ◯ ◯
HOW WELL I DID

# NOTES ON MY DAY

_____

_____

_____

## PRODUCTIVITY RATING

1    2    3    4    5    6    7    8    9    10

Date: / / 20

# MOST IMPORTANT TASK OF THE DAY
If you only complete this then today was still a great day

1. _____  ○ ○ ○ ○ ○
HOW WELL I DID

# TASKS OF SECONDARY IMPORTANCE
Getting these done will make my day even greater

2. _____  ○ ○ ○ ○ ○
HOW WELL I DID

3. _____  ○ ○ ○ ○ ○
HOW WELL I DID

# ADDITIONAL TASKS
Don't tackle these until the ones above are done

4. _____  ○ ○ ○ ○ ○
HOW WELL I DID

5. _____  ○ ○ ○ ○ ○
HOW WELL I DID

# NOTES ON MY DAY

_____

_____

_____

## PRODUCTIVITY RATING

1    2    3    4    5    6    7    8    9    10

# WEEKLY REVIEW

Week of _____

## WEEKLY TRIUMPHS
Want went well this week

_____

_____

_____

## COULD DO BETTER
What fell short of expectations?

_____

_____

_____

## WHAT I'VE LEARNED
Lessons I can grow from

_____

_____

_____

## FOCUS FOR NEXT WEEK
Where I need to spend my energy

_____

_____

Made in United States
Troutdale, OR
09/19/2023

13037457R00086